COACHING Wrestling SUCCESSFULLY

Dan Gable
University of Iowa

Human Kinetics

Library of Congress Cataloging-in-Publication Data

Gable, Dan.
    Coaching wrestling successfully / Dan Gable.
       p.   cm.
    Includes index.
    ISBN 0-87322-404-3 (pbk.)
    1. Wrestling--Coaching.   I. Title.
    GV1196.3.G33   1998
    796.812—dc21   98-20917
                                          CIP

ISBN: 0-87322-404-3

Drawings on pages 64–67 are reprinted, by permission, from M. Alter, 1998, *Sport Stretch* (Champaign, IL: Human Kinetics), 111, 112, 117, 122, 136, 141, 146, 158, 179, 184.

Interior photos provided by **Arizona State University:** p.163 (bottom); **Dan Gable:** p. iii, 4, 7, 9, 60 (bottom); **Nick Gallo:** p. 63; **Iowa State University:** p. 6; **Mitchell Kelly:** p. 191; **Oklahoma State University:** p. 8, 68, 163 (top); **OPI Photo Unit:** p. 41 (left); **Tom Roberts:** 48, 85–123, 130, 133, 136–140, 148, 150–159; **Bob Siddens:** p. vii, 5; **University of Iowa Photo Services:** 16–21, 24, 26–30, 34, 37, 39, 41 (right), 58, 59, 60 (top), 61, 62, 70, 73, 110, 131, 132, 134, 145–147, 149, 172, 175, 179, 190, 203

Managing Editor: Coree Schutter
Copyeditor: Heather Stith
Proofreader: Erin Cler
Indexer: Nan Badgett
Graphic Designer: Nancy Rasmus
Graphic Artist: Francine Hamerski
Photo Editor: Boyd LaFoon
Cover Designer: Jack Davis
Photographer (cover): University of Iowa Photographic Service
Illustrators: Joe Bellis and Kim Maxey (Mac art); Michael Richardson (line art)
Printer: United Graphics

Copies of this book are available at special discounts for bulk purchase for sales promotions, premiums, fund-raising, or educational use. Special editions or book excerpts can also be created to specificiations. For details, contact the Special Sales Manager at Human Kinetics.

Printed in the United States of America   10   9   8   7

Human Kinetics
Web site: www.HumanKinetics.com

United States: Human Kinetics, P.O. Box 5076, Champaign, IL 61825-5076
800-747-4457
e-mail: humank@hkusa.com

Canada: Human Kinetics, 475 Devonshire Road, Unit 100, Windsor, ON N8Y 2L5
800-465-7301 (in Canada only)
e-mail: orders@hkcanada.com

Europe: Human Kinetics, 107 Bradford Road, Stanningley
Leeds LS28 6AT, United Kingdom
+44 (0) 113 255 5665
e-mail: hk@hkeurope.com

Australia: Human Kinetics, 57A Price Avenue, Lower Mitcham, South Australia 5062
08 8277 1555
e-mail: liaw@hkaustralia.com

New Zealand: Human Kinetics, Division of Sports Distributors NZ Ltd.
P.O. Box 300 226 Albany, North Shore City, Auckland
0064 9 448 1207
e-mail: blairc@hknewz.com

Coaching Wrestling Successfully is dedicated to "family." First and foremost, to my immediate family—Dad (Mack), Mom (Katie), sister (Diane), wife (Kathy), and daughters (Jennifer, Annie, Molly, and Mackenzie). Second, to my other family of all my wrestlers, which often included more than one person from their immediate family.

CONTENTS

Part I Coaching Foundation

Part II Coaching Plans

Part III Coaching Skills and Tactics

FOREWORD

The wrestling world views Dan Gable as a legend and superstar. As a wrestler, in high school he won state championships and national championships. In college, he won national championships. Following college, he won world championships and became an Olympic champion. As a coach, Dan Gable had no peer in any collegiate sport. His Iowa teams won 21 straight Big Ten championships and 15 NCAA championships.

While all of these achievements are wonderful and add to my admiration and respect for him, I really don't think of Dan Gable as a wrestling competitor or a wrestling coach. Instead, my thoughts are much the same as they were more than 40 years ago when I first met a young, crew-cut, red-haired lad. I just think of him as Daniel.

As I've traveled all across the country putting on wrestling clinics for coaches, wrestlers, and officials, many people identify me as Dan Gable's high school coach. Inevitably, someone in the group would ask just what Dan was like in the wrestling room. My response to them and my message to you is that I was very fortunate to have Dan in my wrestling room. And I wish you could know Daniel as I know him—a very sincere and sensitive person.

I've had many highlights with Daniel over the years, but I would like to share a couple of the most special ones with you.

When we both went into the National Wrestling Hall of Fame in Oklahoma the same year, Dan asked me to be his presenter. It meant a great deal to me to be his presenter into the Hall of Fame—I've always been proud of all of Dan's accomplishments. I spoke of Dan's loyalty.

When he was in high school at West Waterloo High School, he was a loyal Wahawk; when he wrestled in college at Iowa State, he was a loyal Cyclone; now, at the University of Iowa, he is a Hawkeye through and through.

When the Iowa team won Daniel's last national championships in Cedar Falls in 1997, I was asked by the National Hall of Fame to present the national trophy to Dan, his staff, and his wrestlers. When I went on the platform to make this presentation, I struggled to keep some composure and avoid breaking down from the emotion of the moment. Talking with Daniel later, he admitted feeling the same emotions.

Daniel is a very intense person in whatever he is involved. He is an advocate for wrestling, in part, because of the work ethic necessary to be a successful competitor. Daniel's premise for this is that in life and wrestling, anything worthwhile comes hard—is achieved at a price.

Dan Gable and Bob Siddens after Iowa's 1997 National championship.

Daniel is also a very firm believer in togetherness. His wonderful rapport with his young men is a by-product of this emphasis. In the same way, Daniel places great importance on his role as a strong family man, both as a husband to his wife, Kathy, and as a father to his four lovely daughters.

Reading *Coaching Wrestling Successfully* will give you a better understanding of Daniel, his philosophy, teaching methods, techniques, and competitive drive. Whether you're a coach, wrestler, parent, or fan, this book offers many valuable lessons from the wrestling legend, who I'm even more proud to know as a special person—Daniel.

Bob Siddens

Former Champion Iowa Wrestlers Talk About Coach Gable

"Dan taught me what excellence was all about. He would watch films to study all opponents, train like a lunatic, and continually educate himself in all aspects of competition and training. He would not let anything get in the way of being the best, and infused his program and the people in it with his powerful aura of excellence. The example he set in his life gave me the direction to be a world champion and obtain an Ivy League law degree. When I see individuals and institutions fail at achieving their goals, it's always because they did not follow the simple rules of commitment to excellence that Dan taught and lived by. Having argued with, been coached by, and wrestled with Dan over the six years I was at Iowa, I can tell you two things for certain: first, no matter what stories you hear about Dan Gable, they in no way express the magnitude of, or do justice to, this human being in terms of his positive effect on people and his greatness; second, I consider myself one of the luckiest human beings on this planet to have experienced Dan Gable as a coach."

Chris Campbell, 3-time Big Ten champion, 2-time NCAA champion,
4-time national freestyle wrestling champion, 4-time World Cup champion,
World wrestling champion, Olympic bronze medallist

"While at Iowa many athletes from other institutions would approach me and ask what the secret of our success was and I had two words for them, "Hard Work." That is what Dan Gable taught us. He taught us that there are no short cuts, no magic tricks, but hard work, dedication, and focus. Dan Gable emphasized all of these things. By Dan Gable putting us through workouts we knew that as athletes we never had to worry about conditioning, strength, or technical skills. The only thing we had to think about was wrestling and that is what Dan Gable taught us to do best. Dan was the type of individual that would go through the same workout as the athletes would do, and as athletes we appreciated that and it made us that much more of a believer in Dan Gable as a coach."

Barry Davis, 4-time Big Ten champion, 3-time NCAA champion, 4-time All-American,
World Championships bronze medallist, Olympic silver medallist

"The influences Dan Gable has had on my career and life are that I should compete while I am prepared properly, and a properly prepared career leads to a well-prepared life. A special characteristic that makes Gable the great coach that he is, is how he reads each individual. He realizes that each athlete is different so he coaches them to their own needs. How he can read an athlete and know what they need is just amazing. I've never seen a man so well known as a legend. When people talk about wrestling they talk about Dan Gable, and the best thing is that it is all good. The secret to his success is preparedness, which is mainly hard work."

Mark Ironside, 4-time Big Ten champion, 3-time Big Ten Athlete of the Year,
Big Ten outstanding wrestler, 4-time All-American, 2-time NCAA champion,
winner of 1998 Dan Hodge Award

"Coach Gable's influence has created a sweeping effect on the sport of wrestling and beyond. His standards as an athlete and coach are unprecedented. Consistent victories are inspired by confidence. This undoubting confidence comes through the Gable training method—OUTWORK THEM ALL. Coach Gable has a special ability to decipher the code of each individual's mind, and not only interpret this code but also communicate and motivate in it. I feel as though I have a special relationship with Dan Gable. Everyone who knows him feels this way."

Lincoln McIlravy, *3-time Big Ten champion, 3-time NCAA champion, NCAA outstanding wrestler, 2-time U.S. Open champion, U.S. Open outstanding wrestler, World Cup champion*

"Now still competing as an athlete and looking to coach in the future in the sport of wrestling, I reflect back on my days under Gable to see how he would have handled certain situations. Coach Gable is a man that truly leads by example. Day in and day out he was at the arena from 7:00 or 8:00 in the morning until 7:00 or 8:00 at night. It showed everyone else the price it takes to be successful. I don't believe anyone in the sport has or will ever have an impact like Coach Gable has. The thing that makes him so different than other coaches is that everyone respects him, not only for what he has accomplished but for the type of person he is. People may not like him, but they have to respect him. Coaches would always come to Iowa to try and figure out what he did differently—what his secret to success was. It was just hard work, but like Gable always said, most people do not know what hard work is."

Troy Steiner, *3-time Big Ten champion, NCAA champion, 4-time All-American, World Cup champion, Pan American champion*

"Gable is the reason I wanted to come to Iowa, he has been like a second father to me in every aspect of life. He gets you motivated and knows just what you need. Just when you think you've got him all figured out he will do something that will surprise you and push you past your breaking point. I think Gable truly sets the standard for the rest of the wrestling world to judge themselves by. The secret to Gable's success is his work ethic and his ability to get his athletes motivated to rise to the occasion."

Joe Williams, *2-time Big Ten champion, 4-time All-American, 3-time national champion*

"As a competitor, Dan Gable taught me to never give up on myself. As a coach, he has taught me to never give up on any of our wrestlers."

Jim Zalesky, *3-time Big Ten champion, 3-time NCAA champion, 4-time All-American*

ACKNOWLEDGMENTS

Many who pursued excellence and took the challenge are in my heart, for their contributions and personal touches were vital. Thanks to all!

All-Americans From the Gable Era

1977
John Bowlsby (5th, Hwt)
Chris Campbell (1st, 177)
Mike DeAnna (3rd, 167)
Mike McGivern (4th, 158)
Keith Mourlam (2nd, 126)

1978
John Bowlsby (5th, Hwt)
Mike DeAnna (6th, 167)
Dan Glenn (3rd, 118)
Bruce Kinseth (2nd, 150)
Randy Lewis (2nd, 126)
Scott Trizzino (3rd, 142)

1979
Mike DeAnna (2nd, 167)
Dan Glenn (3rd, 118)
* Bruce Kinseth (1st, 150)
Randy Lewis (1st, 126)
Bud Palmer (2nd, 177)
Scott Trizzino (2nd, 142)

1980
Doug Anderson (8th, 167)
Ed Banach (1st, 177)
Dan Glenn (2nd, 118)
Randy Lewis (1st, 134)
King Mueller (3rd, 150)
Dean Phinney (3rd, Hwt)
Mark Stevenson (7th, 158)
Lennie Zalesky (4th, 142)

1981
Ed Banach (1st, 177)
Lou Banach (1st, Hwt)
Barry Davis (7th, 118)

Mike DeAnna (2nd, 167)
Randy Lewis (7th, 134)
Tim Riley (7th, 126)
Scott Trizzino (2nd, 150)
Jim Zalesky (5th, 158)
Lennie Zalesky (2nd, 142)

1982
Ed Banach (2nd, 177)
Lou Banach (3rd, Hwt)
Pete Bush (1st, 190)
Barry Davis (1st, 118)
Dave Fitzgerald (7th, 167)
Jeff Kerber (6th, 134)
Jim Zalesky (1st, 158)
Lennie Zalesky (2nd, 142)

1983
Ed Banach (1st, 190)
Lou Banach (1st, Hwt)
Barry Davis (1st, 126)
Duane Goldman (2nd, 177)
Jim Heffernan (4th, 150)
Jeff Kerber (5th, 134)
Harlan Kistler (3rd, 142)
Tim Riley (5th, 118)
Jim Zalesky (1st, 158)

1984
Duane Goldman (2nd, 177)
Jeff Kerber (6th, 142)
Lindley Kistler (2nd, 167)
Marty Kistler (2nd, 150)
Greg Randall (2nd, 134)
Tim Riley (5th, 118)
Mark Trizzino (4th, 126)
* Jim Zalesky (1st, 158)

1985
* Barry Davis (1st, 126)
Rico Chiapparelli (5th, 177)
Kevin Dresser (4th, 142)
Matt Egeland (2nd, 118)
Duane Goldman (2nd, 190)
Jim Heffernan (2nd, 150)
Lindley Kistler (5th, 167)
Marty Kistler (1st, 158)
Greg Randall (5th, 134)

1986
Royce Alger (5th, 158)
Rico Chiapparelli (4th, 177)
Kevin Dresser (1st, 142)
Duane Goldman (1st, 190)
Jim Heffernan (1st, 150)
* Marty Kistler (1st, 167)
Brad Penrith (1st, 126)
Greg Randall (2nd, 134)

1987
Royce Alger (1st, 167)
Rico Chiapparelli (1st, 177)
Jim Heffernan (2nd, 150)
John Heffernan (6th, 158)
Brad Penrith (2nd, 126)
Mark Sindlinger (4th, Hwt)

1988
Royce Alger (1st, 177)
John Heffernan (4th, 158)
Joe Melchiore (2nd, 134)
Brad Penrith (2nd, 126)
Mark Sindlinger (6th, Hwt)

1989
Tom Brands (4th, 126)
Steve Martin (7th, 118)
Joe Melchiore (3rd, 134)
Mark Reiland (4th, 158)

1990
Terry Brands (1st, 126)
Tom Brands (1st, 134)
Bart Chelesvig (3rd, 167)
Brooks Simpson (2nd, 190)
Troy Steiner (5th, 142)
Doug Streicher (6th, 150)

1991
Terry Brands (2nd, 126)
Tom Brands (1st, 134)
Bart Chelesvig (3rd, 177)
Travis Fiser (6th, 190)
Mark Reiland (1st, 167)
Tom Ryan (2nd, 158)
Terry Steiner (3rd, 150)
Troy Steiner (2nd, 142)
Chad Zaputil (2nd, 118)

1992
Terry Brands (1st, 126)
* Tom Brands (1st, 134)

Bart Chelesvig (3rd, 177)
Travis Fiser (5th, 190)
John Oostendorp (5th, Hwt)
Tom Ryan (3rd, 158)
Terry Steiner (5th, 150)
Troy Steiner (1st, 142)
Chad Zaputil (2nd, 118)

1993
Ray Brinzer (3rd, 177)
Lincoln McIlravy (1st, 142)
John Oostendorp (3rd, Hwt)
Joel Sharratt (2nd, 190)
* Terry Steiner (1st, 150)
Troy Steiner (3rd, 134)
Chad Zaputil (2nd, 118)

1994
Lincoln McIlravy (1st, 150)
Jeff McGinness (5th, 126)
Mike Mena (7th, 118)
Joel Sharratt (1st, 190)
Daryl Weber (6th, 142)
Joe Williams (7th, 158)

1995
Ray Brinzer (3rd, 177)
Mark Ironside (6th, 134)

Jeff McGinness (1st, 126)
Lincoln McIlravy (2nd, 150)
Mike Mena (3rd, 118)
Matt Nerem (6th, 167)
Joel Sharratt (2nd, 190)
Daryl Weber (6th, 158)
Bill Zadick (5th, 142)

1996
Lee Fullhart (4th, 195)
Mike Mena (5th, 118)
Mark Ironside (3rd, 134)
Mike Uker (8th, 150)
Joe Williams (1st, 158)
Daryl Weber (1st, 167)
Bill Zadick (1st, 142)

1997
Lee Fullhart (1st, 190)
Kasey Gilliss (6th, 142)
Mark Ironside (1st, 134)
* Lincoln McIlravy (1st, 150)
Mike Mena (2nd, 126)
Mike Uker (5th, 167)
Jessie Whitmer (1st, 118)
Joe Williams (1st, 158)

* Outstanding wrestler at NCAA meet. National champions are in boldface.

**Also, a special thanks to Kristen Payne and Dan Foster
for supplying nutritional information on pages 68-72.**

INTRODUCTION

I wrote this book to share what I believe are the keys to success in coaching and wrestling. It's for you—the wrestling coach, the wrestler, and the wrestling fan. It's for those who want to improve their standing in a chosen endeavor, whether they're trying to build the top wrestling program or trying to become the top wrestler in their weight class.

Wrestling is about individual achievement. I'm a big believer in starting with high standards and raising them; I don't believe in lowering standards in order to make things more competitive. We make progress only when we push ourselves to the highest level. If we don't progress, we backslide into bad habits, laziness, and poor attitude. A hard-working attitude is an essential ingredient for success, no matter how scientific or sophisticated wrestling becomes. Success in wrestling is more than just winning; it's determined by many other factors. But I'll concede that winning is probably the most fun.

This book is about achieving success through hard work, a positive mental approach, and experience. The hard work must come from you. In the following pages, I'll share my thoughts and experiences. And maybe along the way we'll both have some fun.

Part 1

COACHING FOUNDATION

Chapter

1

DEVELOPING A WRESTLING COACHING PHILOSOPHY

In the introduction to this book, I said that the only way a coach or wrestler will improve is by setting increasingly high standards and then working hard to achieve them. That's something I believe in strongly. It's a big part of my coaching philosophy. Another big part of my philosophy is that champions are often, but not always, the ones who win the most matches. In coaching or competing on the mat, true champions are the guys who get the most out of themselves and others; they strive to be great, and they often achieve greatness. At the least, they command respect.

What's your philosophy? Have you taken time to define it? If you haven't thought much about it, now's the time to start. A philosophy is like a mental steering mechanism. It guides you in the decisions you make. If you don't have one or if yours is faulty, you'll go nowhere or get lost trying to get somewhere. If you have an effective one, not only can you achieve a desired destination, but you can help others reach it too. I believe that we coaches must have a positive philosophy. If we do, we can be successful, and we can help our wrestlers achieve success too. A favorite quote of mine by Rafe sums it up best: "Whatever you most need in life, the best way for you to get it is to help someone else get it who needs it even more than you do."

THE SEEDS OF A PHILOSOPHY

We all began developing our philosophies early in life. My emphasis on hard work began taking shape at an early age. My parents, Mack and Katie, were always passing along words of wisdom, often in the form of catchy motivational phrases—the kind

My parents (Mack and Katie) were the biggest influence on me, giving me the guidance and opportunities I needed to excel in life and wrestling. The death of my sister, Diane, when I was 15 was also a motivating factor for me.

of slogans coaches put on gym and locker room walls. Even today I spend a lot of time reading and studying the motivational phrases my parents used to inspire me as a kid.

I was fortunate in how I was brought up. My childhood memories are good ones. My parents gave me the opportunity to be very successful by guiding and supporting me as well as giving me little pushes when needed. For example, on my 10th birthday I received a set of weights for a present. After a few days, my mom pointed out that I still hadn't touched them. She said "Those new weights you'd been asking for, they seem to be staying pretty new. You know, they might get a little rusty just sitting there." The weights were put to use soon after that not-so-subtle reminder from Mom.

People and events we encounter during childhood have a lasting effect. We have to understand that fact about ourselves and our athletes. Kids from good families have a leg up on life. They're taught good values and are usually self-disciplined, but not everyone is so lucky. Many kids must look outside the home for direction. Fortunately, there are organizations that provide a positive alternative or support for the family's philosophical base. From the ages of 4 to 12, the local YMCA played a big part in my development. The Y

taught me many important values and sparked my natural competitiveness. It also helped shape my philosophy.

THE SHAPING OF A PHILOSOPHY

After those early childhood days in which parents or significant others give much of the meaning you have about the world, you enter another phase of philosophical development. At this stage, classmates and teammates, teachers and coaches, books, and competitive experiences do much to shape your outlook.

By the Book

Two great resources that I read while growing up had a profound effect on my perspective. One was *The Edge* by Howard Ferguson, the former great coach at St. Edward's High School in Ohio. Another one of my favorites was *The Heart of a Champion* by Bob Richards, the 1952 and 1956 Olympic pole vault champion. Besides stressing the importance of attitude to achieve greatness in sport, Richards emphasized the spiritual side of life. His book strengthened my belief in spirituality as the building block to every meaningful achievement.

The Influence of Coaches

Anyone who has played sports knows what an impact a coach can have, good or bad. If you're a wrestling coach, you probably had a special coach who made you think that coaching was a special profession. On the other hand, we've all had or seen coaches who are just the opposite; they turn kids off to the sport and hurt our profession. The philosophies of my former coaches and now coaching colleagues had a great impression on me. They have been the foundation for my success as a coach.

My high school coach at West Waterloo, Bob Siddens, had a big influence on my philosophy as an athlete and as a coach. During his Hall-of-Fame career, Bob took kids from all walks of life and helped them develop on and off the mat. He treated us as individuals, respecting our personality differences. Yet he knew how to get all of us to strive to be our best and to sacrifice for the good of the team. Bob's philosophy on competing was, "Win with humility, lose with dignity, *but don't lose.*" Perhaps most important of all, everyone who wrestled under Coach Siddens knew that he had their best interests in mind in every action he took.

The 95-Pound Problem

I began my high school wrestling career at West Waterloo thinking I'd wrestle at the 103-pound spot, but the team needed a strong 95-pounder. Coach Siddens told me that if I made the lower weight, the spot was mine. I wouldn't even have to try out. Being a first-year team member, I couldn't pass up the guaranteed position. But after making the weight a few times, I started feeling sorry for myself. My focus was on self-pity rather than getting the job done.

Knowing that I was a highly motivated person, Coach Siddens challenged me and told me to quit being a baby about wrestling at 95. That's all it took for me to get going and to have a good season. If another team member had been acting the way I was, Bob would have handled the situation differently—in the manner that best suited the wrestler's personality.

A great high school coach will continue the learning process needed away from home that parents can't give. Bob Siddens, my high school coach, did that for me.

In college at Iowa State, I drew upon the philosophy of my coach, Harold Nichols. Coach Nichols provided an environment for success, one that bred wrestling champions. He believed that great wrestlers made other wrestlers great. My experiences in his practice room taught me many lessons about the value of competition. To this day, I believe that wrestling greatness is achieved only through training that makes you push yourself to survive.

Many other coaches influenced my philosophy. Doug Blubaugh, a 1960 Olympic champion, taught me a lot about self-discipline. Doug grew up in a lifestyle that demanded a hard work ethic. Every day he did farm chores early each morning, ran five miles into school, attended classes all day, went to wrestling practice and outworked everyone on the team, ran back home, worked on the farm until dark, and then did his homework before bed. This example of self-discipline had a lot to do with my training and my philosophy about what it

takes to excel. Doug's wrestling style was just as unique as his amazing work ethic. Doug couldn't see very well, but that didn't keep him from using a straightforward, aggressive style. One time I saw Doug wrestle right into the first row of bleachers, and people say that he once even tackled a referee by mistake.

Myron Roderick, an ex-Oklahoma State wrestler and coach, is another person who helped shape my outlook. He taught me that politics play a part in wrestling, just as they do in other sports and organizations. Myron also taught me how to adapt to the situation. He was a master of wrestling technique; he not only knew the moves, he also knew when to make them.

Bill Weick, a two-time NCAA champion and coach, and Jim Peckham, both 1972 Olympic team assistant coaches, gave me insights into what it takes to build a successful program (see chapter 4). They showed me the importance of providing a positive social setting for the team where the wrestlers could grow

A great college coach will help make moving away from home simpler because independence isn't too far away. My college coach, Harold Nichols (right), did exactly that.

together outside the practice room. Another thing that Bill and Jim shared with me was their intense love for wrestling. I think they are the only people who understand how I feel when I watch wrestling.

Finally, I must mention Bill Farrell, my 1972 Olympic coach. Part businessman, part wrestling coach, Bill found a way to fulfill the needs of each member of the team. He taught me how to make full use of the resources available and how to acquire additional resources as they are needed. He got things accomplished whenever and wherever needed.

Saving the Gold

At the 1969 World Championships, because the mark scoring system was being used, U.S. wrestler Fred Fozzard had to await the outcome of a match between a Soviet and a Bulgarian to determine his fate. Fozzard's coach, Bill Farrell, learned that one of the communist block wrestlers was going to throw the match to prevent Fozzard from winning. Farrell warned the officials before the match began. Sure enough, one of the wrestlers took a dive. But because of Farrell's warning, the officials disqualified both of the communist wrestlers and awarded the gold to Fozzard.

The Influence of Wrestlers

Being involved in wrestling, we have all seen competitors that we especially admired. They provide models for coaches to point out to our own athletes, and they provide inspiration and direction to other wrestlers. I had the honor and benefit of learning from some great wrestlers who were just a bit older than I. They taught me a lot about wrestling, but they also had a profound impact on my coaching philosophy.

Bob Buzzard, a former East Waterloo and Iowa State wrestling star, had a quick and explosive style. He was great at changing

Attitude and work ethic are what Olympic champion and World coach Doug Blubaugh (shown here with me) had while competing and coaching; yet I must mention that his feared front headlock was brutal.

Myron Roderick (standing) has been successful at all levels of the sport—a great wrestler, a great coach, and now president of the U.S. Wrestling Hall of Fame.

speeds during a match, knowing how to keep the opponent off-guard. Tom Peckham, who starred at Cresco High School and Iowa State University, was what I call a grinder. He wasn't flashy, but he got the job done. Tom used his physical style and leverage to wear down his opponents.

Buzzard and Peckham had two contrasting styles that I respected. By watching them, I learned that no single style is best for every wrestler. I keep this fact in mind when I coach. My approach is to allow the athletes to use the style that works best for them. That doesn't mean that I'll permit them to use poor fundamentals or use a lot of high-risk moves that rarely work. But it does mean that I don't try to make them change to some ideal wrestling style.

I'm also a firm believer in a physical style of wrestling. This style requires wrestlers to be highly disciplined in their training. Perhaps the hardest aspect of the physical style is that it contradicts human nature, which is to use the easiest method possible. Being a physical type wrestler has hard work written all over it, and it takes a special athlete to master it, but it's not impossible. Even less physical wrestlers can benefit from using a physical wrestling style in certain situations.

The Always-Developing Philosophy

Getting set in your ways is okay for some things, but as a coach, you should always be examining and, if necessary, improving your philosophy. Making the transition from athlete to coach was easier for me than most because my personality allowed others to be themselves. Like Bob Siddens, I understood the individual differences in my athletes and never thought it was appropriate to change them without taking many things into account. But in the past, being too flexible has backfired. A few years ago, I made the mistake of giving my athletes too much freedom, when I should have instead stepped in and taken control.

Talent Only Goes So Far

My 1982–83 recruits were the highest rated recruiting class of my career. They had an extraordinary amount of talent, so I thought I could afford to loosen the reins a little. Before long, this group of talented wrestlers helped the team lose its competitive edge. They didn't demonstrate the discipline needed to be the best, and their attitude rubbed off on the less-talented wrestlers on the team. Soon, the team's actions on and off the mat were having ramifications that would cost the wrestling program for several years to come. I have to take responsibility for not taking charge of the situation before it got out of hand.

Don't get caught up in winning only and be willing to compromise the good values in your program. Less than great attitudes and activities can ruin even the best of programs. Sometimes coaches need a few bad experiences to keep them on track or to make changes for the better. If you do make a mistake, learn from it and avoid letting it happen again.

The great majority of people and experiences I've encountered throughout my wrestling and coaching career have been positive. Yours probably have been too. I hope that my sharing with you some of the people and events who started, shaped, and continued to develop my coaching philosophy gives you some ideas that will help you better define your philosophy.

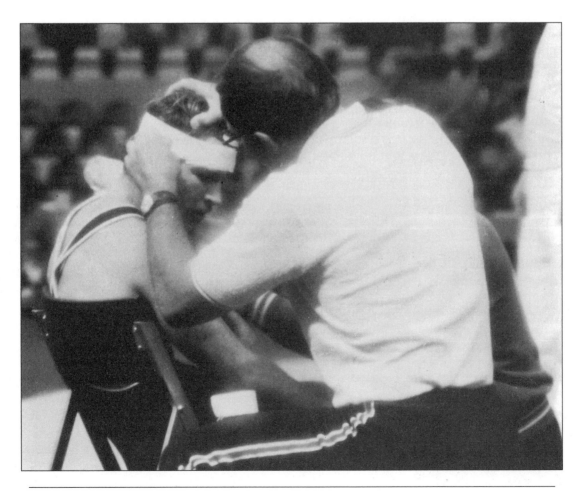

My relationship with Bill Farrell expanded beyond competition—I have worked with him and Asics for the last quarter of a century. Here, Bill Farrell and Bill Weick are figuring out a way to keep me from getting disqualified due to a blood distraction. Thanks!

FROM PHILOSOPHY TO REALITY

A wrestling program is people. That's who it starts with; that's who it ends with. The most important people are your coaching staff and your wrestlers. Also important are the parents, relatives, fans, administrators, people of the community, and in my case, as part of a public institution, all the citizens of Iowa. I'll talk more in the next chapter about what to keep in mind when communicating with all of these different groups. Given that people are the backbone of a program, the philosophy you adopt should be people-centered. By that I mean that the approach you take should be in the best interest of your athletes and others associated with the program.

If your philosophy is sound, the challenge is to see that you and your wrestlers embody that philosophy. Meeting that challenge involves setting specific expectations about behaviors for individuals and the team. Realize that all eyes are focused upon you, the head coach. A successful coach cannot get by with "Practice what I preach, not what I do." You set the tone for the program. If your philosophy is the mental steering mechanism, then your behavior is the tangible element,

the nuts and bolts, that determines whether you are on course. Live by the standards you set. Be a good example.

Academics

You have to know where your athletes are heading in their academic pursuits. Being successful in academics comes first; wrestling comes second. High school coaches need to keep up on college entrance requirements and advise athletes accordingly. Core courses, college entrance exams, and GPAs should be important concerns for you and your wrestlers. Also, encourage your athletes to seek advice from guidance and academic counselors at your school. In short, do all you can to emphasize academics so that your athletes succeed academically.

Excellence

When an athlete enters my program, we discuss his ideal objective: receiving straight A's and going undefeated in wrestling. Then we discuss the opposite extreme, flunking out and never winning. After discussing both scenarios, I show the athlete the graph illustrated in figure 1.1. This graph is used to

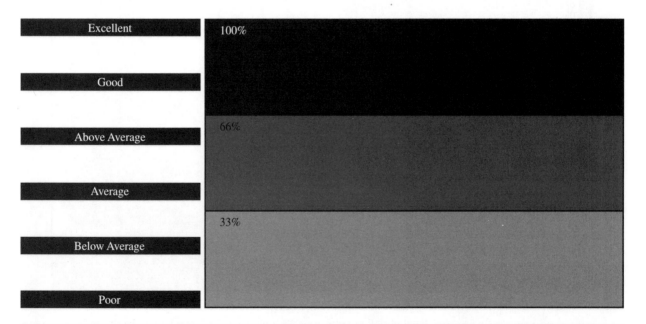

Figure 1.1   Levels of excellence

explain to them the level they need to achieve in comparison to their opposition. I expect the athletes in my program to be at the top of the graph, to be dominant. Because I am straight with them up front, the athletes have no doubts about my expectations. They make an informed choice about continuing or quitting the program.

This graph may seem harsh, and it may not be appropriate at lower levels of wrestling. At the Division I college level, however, it's necessary and in the best interest of your athletes and yourself. You can both keep from wasting a lot of time by deciding that the expectations aren't something that the athlete feels comfortable with. After all, your professional life hinges on the output of the wrestlers on your team. If your athletes can't meet the standards you've set, then for the sake of your coaching future it's probably best that they decide to drop off the team. Not all of them need to be great wrestlers, but they all must be on the same page in terms of having an attitude that's essential to success.

Teamwork

Your team will be only as successful as the sum of its individual parts. The great wrestling programs don't maintain their level by relying on just one or two wrestlers. In order to get to the top, you have to get a group of student-athletes to work together for a common purpose. On the other hand, one great wrestler can give your program a great deal of visibility and credibility. Then the coach must take the next step and increase the overall level of performance of every spot on the team. When the level of team success is high, you can concentrate more on the development of individuals. But if the program begins to slip, then it's important to begin stressing team objectives again.

SUMMARY

You are the only person who can establish a philosophy for your program, but your philosophy must be a positive one in order for your wrestling program to achieve greatness. To recap, here is the approach I suggest:

- Keep in mind that champions aren't always the ones who win the most matches.
- Establish a philosophy that is in the best interest of your athletes now and when they leave the program.
- Set high standards and be willing to work to achieve them.
- Incorporate beliefs, attitudes, and behaviors from the things you read and other successful wrestling coaches and wrestlers that have impressed you.
- Emphasize to your athletes the importance of having priorities based on a strong faith, family, academics, and athletics.
- Identify and set objectives for yourself, your wrestlers individually, and your team.

Chapter
2

COMMUNICATING YOUR APPROACH

In the first chapter I talked about how critical it is to determine what's important to you. Without a philosophy, and the goals and objectives that stem from it, you can't achieve much in wrestling. Once you know what you want to accomplish, you must be able to motivate others to strive for the same thing in order to make it happen. That's where communication comes in.

When I began my coaching career, I didn't come across well in the first few meetings with the wrestlers, which was a problem because first impressions are crucial. I didn't like to speak in front of groups. But as a coach, a big part of my job involved instructing and motivating my wrestling team. In addition, boosters, fans, various civic groups, and the media expected me to speak. I had only two options: become a better communicator or get out of coaching. You know what I chose.

Some of you may be smooth talkers, naturals before an audience. Maybe you do better in one-on-one conversations by making good eye contact with the other person and effectively sending and receiving messages. More likely, you have a little trouble in both situations. Do your wrestlers often misinterpret what you said? Do they respond positively to what you intend to be motivational messages? Do you take time to observe and listen to them so you can respond effectively to them?

Nobody expects you to be a perfect communicator, but you must communicate well enough to be the best coach you can be and to help your athletes be their best. After you determine what you need to improve, work on it; don't avoid it. Being able to share your knowledge, your discipline, and your dreams is essential for good leadership. Use the information in this chapter to learn how to be a more effective communicator, leader, and coach.

IMPROVING YOUR COMMUNICATION SKILLS

Communicating, like a lot of other skills, takes practice. Knowing the guidelines to good communication doesn't help if you aren't going to use them. When I began working on my communication skills, I did so in small groups that I felt comfortable with. I recommend this approach. You are less afraid of sounding awkward, so you feel more free to talk. You can therefore focus more on what you are saying and how it is being interpreted than on self-conscious thoughts.

Speaking in small, familiar groups should help you boost your confidence about speaking to larger and less familiar groups. Before rushing into that type of situation, however, do some preparation. For instance, tag along with another coach or friend who is an accomplished speaker to his or her next speaking engagement. Watch how that person prepares and then delivers the presentation, and then try to incorporate the parts of the speaker's approach that you think will work well for you into your next speech.

A Lesson in Presentation

In my later days as an athlete and early days in the coaching profession, I went to observe and listen to a Bob Richards presentation at my old high school (West Waterloo). Bob's speech made a big impression, giving me insights on how to entertain and speak to groups in the future. During his presentation, he recalled real-life success stories. Many of the people Bob cited were familiar to me, but I wasn't aware of some of the unique circumstances that they had to conquer to be so successful. Bob's delivery and details produced powerful images of the individuals and their achievements.

Being Yourself

Learning from excellent communicators is a great idea, but copying them never works.

There is no one type of personality for a wrestling coach (or a wrestler for that matter), yet wrestling does weed out those who try to be something they're not. In that way, wrestling is one of the most honest sports; there's no hiding. Don't think you can fool your team. Can you imagine me trying to act calm and reserved, sitting quietly in my coaching chair during a match? My wrestlers would know I was churning on the inside, no matter how nonchalant I looked. Instead, try to be the best communicator you can be within your style and personality. Very simply, be yourself as good as you can be.

A great benefit to being yourself is that it helps others to trust you. If a wrestler has a problem, he's more likely to come to you for help if he knows he's going to be dealt with honestly. Another benefit to being honest is that you won't get yourself caught in a lie. If you are always trying to manipulate others with some false persona, sooner or later the real you will be exposed, which will probably hurt the relationships you've built on the phony persona you're projecting. So shoot straight—you and your program will be better off if you do.

Gaining and Maintaining Respect

Your communications will have a much greater impact if others involved in the program respect you, but respect isn't automatically given to a coach. Just like wrestlers, coaches have to earn whatever respect they get. The best way to begin earning that respect is by being sincere; this real you will represent what you want to communicate to those inside and outside of the program.

I'm fortunate in that many people automatically respect Dan Gable even though they may not really know me. The '72 Olympics, the record number of NCAA championships, and other visible achievements in my career have helped me get the recognition and respect that most other coaches would love to have. But the type of respect that is built on win-loss records and fame is not real respect. Real respect is earned among the people who really know you.

Gable,

How's the hip? Probably hurts like the rest of your body. This must be your body telling you to rest and recoup (listen to it). Hope your family is doing well and has a good holiday. Hope Kathy doesn't spend too much for your sake. Anyway, I heard you were laid up, so I thought instead of a call you could read this in your free time, not that you have much of that. Congratulations on the Penn State victory. I heard Fullhart had a close match? Probably a good idea to hold off on the Hand-McCoy match. We won our first dual 81-0. We will be tested more this weekend.

Feels great to be doing something I love and get paid for it. I owe that to you! I'm learning how to deal with individuals and trying to get their potential out of them, but I'm still learning how to push the right buttons. I figure that's something you have to always keep learning. I feel what I learned from you gives me a huge advantage. I know how to work them hard but I need to learn how to train them from a peaking point. What I learned from you, I hope, is that reinventing practices and workouts will help improve their skills and still keep their wrestling intense and tough <u>the way it is supposed to be!</u>

Gable, I don't mean to get personal or stupid. I just am very thankful and feel lucky to have been able to spend time under you as a wrestler. I have to say I am sorry to you and Jimmy and myself for not winning a national title or even a U.S. Open. Never in my life have I ever won anything worth talking about. I don't cry about it and I never want anyone to feel sorry for me because of it. But what hurts is letting down you, Jimmy, and especially my dad. I had dreams where I won that national title and it was an incredible feeling. I even knew I was dreaming and didn't want to wake up. I look back now and wonder what would have happened if I did win. I guess I'll never know. But I have to think that if I would've, I might be out of wrestling. What a terrible thought because I really love coaching. I wish it was college but I feel there is work to be done here. I don't know what winning the big one for me would've done, but I know what losing has done (I don't like it), but I am learning from it and I will do everything to prevent it from happening as a coach to my athletes. I hope to treat them as well as you have treated me. I always enjoyed the journey to the top even though I didn't get there. Sometimes I think if I would have gotten there I wouldn't get to enjoy another climb. Looking back that is ridiculous.

Every year is different. I hope to instill that in my wrestlers. Whether or not I compete, I can say I am busy worrying about this team and its future. If I do step on the mat again I will give my best potential.

Anyway, I don't mean to make this letter troublesome, but rather a tribute to you and what you have done for me. I am not a very open person and I don't expect a couple of pages to cover what I've learned from you. Rarely there is a day that goes by that I don't think of how you would do something that I have learned from you. You're a stand-up guy Dan Gable. I am forever in your debt. If the kids I coach can walk away from this program feeling the way I felt about your program, I know I will have done a good job. I wish you and your family the best! I hope after the season you can get out and do some fishing down around my way in Marengo or at least get yourself out somewhere enjoying the outdoors. You've earned it!

Always climbing,

Travis

P.S. Think healthy!

Providing a Leading Example

Be a positive example for your athletes. If you want your wrestlers to be dedicated and disciplined, then you have to lead the way. Ideally you'll have athletes in your program who will provide a similar, positive model for their teammates. If not, then your example will have to do until you establish leaders on the team. Once you get some leaders, typically upperclassmen, their leadership often rubs off on some of the younger wrestlers, who in time develop into leaders themselves.

While making the transition from athlete to coach early in my career at the University of Iowa, I was faced with many new problems.

One of the most glaring problems was the absence of leaders on the team. At Iowa State, West Waterloo High School, and on national teams I had taken the presence of great leadership for granted. The following are just a few of the differences I noticed when I first started coaching at Iowa:

1. The wrestling room was basically off-limits outside of regular practice time. I was used to the wrestling room staying open and nearly always being in use.

2. Wrestlers who lost at two- and three-day tournaments disappeared from the site after they were eliminated. I was

As long as a team has leaders like Mark Ironside, other team members will have no excuse for not knowing what it takes.

used to wrestlers staying and studying the championship matches of their competitors. Of course most were in the championship matches anyway.

3. Wrestlers competed tougher against easier opponents than they did against strong competition. I was used to wrestlers going all out, no matter whom they were wrestling.

One of my first lessons as a coach was that talent is everywhere, but a winning attitude is not. For the first couple of years at Iowa, I had to fill the leadership void on the team. Eventually, the leadership issue was straightened out, and the University of Iowa wrestling program has had a string of great leaders ever since.

Educating Your Athletes

In Part III I'll describe how to teach wrestlers specific techniques and tactics, a crucial skill for any coach. You can also educate athletes in many other areas through effective communication. For example, you can express very clearly to them what is and is not acceptable conduct on and off the mat, and you can

help them learn how to take better care of their bodies. These two seemingly simple lessons on the importance of proper self-conduct and physical maintenance can benefit your program and be of life-long benefit to your athletes. Don't let those opportunities for teaching pass you by.

Keeping a Comfortable Distance

How close do you get to your wrestlers? You want them to trust you and to feel free to confide in you, but how much should you confide in them? There's a fine line between sharing a good, healthy relationship with your athletes and getting too close to them. Maintaining some distance has its advantages. The athletes won't expect any special favors or leniency when they let the program down, nor will they take you for granted, as they might if you are always in close contact with them.

Because of my individual accomplishments as a wrestler and my program's success, many wrestlers are almost in awe of me when they enter the program. That sense of awe may not last long, but the certain aura it creates helps me and my wrestlers from getting too involved in each other's personal lives. Yet it does not prevent us from communicating well with one another and working out problems when they arise.

One such problem occurred the morning everyone was to meet in the locker room before the 5:45 a.m. flight to Michigan for the 1982 Big Ten Championships. When Dave Fitzgerald, the team's 167-pounder, arrived, he found a note taped to his locker. The note was from Barry Davis, the team's 118-pounder who was ranked the #1 wrestler in the country at the time. It read:

Dear Dave,

I feel that you can relate to what I'm doing [because Dave had been involved in a similar incident earlier]. I tried making weight earlier in the day and just couldn't do it. Therefore, I'm not going to go to the Big Ten's with the team. I do want to wish everybody the best of luck at the tournament and at nationals. Don't try to find me because I'm going to be hiding out and impossible to find.

Good Luck,

Barry

Obviously, this was a major problem that I needed to address quickly. Good communication was the key to resolving it.

I talked to his teammates, and they said that Barry had gone to work out at 3:30 in the morning. I then called a few of the nonstarters to form a search party to find him. Next, I got a hold of the night security officers who were able to provide the times that Barry entered and exited the workout facility. In addition, I spoke with his roommates who gave me some ideas where Barry had been spending time.

I started my search in a remote area of Iowa City where one of Barry's friends lived. I didn't have the exact address, so I stopped at a local grocery store to check the phone book. When I entered the store, I saw Barry at the checkout counter with a bag full of junk food. Our eyes met, and he dropped the bag and said "I haven't eaten a thing yet."

A lot of Barry Davis's competitive career might have been jeopardized if a good system of communication had not been in place.

I didn't know what to expect, so I blocked the doorway in case Barry tried to run. But we just talked for a minute. I told him that I knew about his weight problem and that I would still like him to make the trip. That was all he needed to hear. Soon both of us were rushing to the plane to get to Ann Arbor in time. Barry made weight with the help of a workout at the Marriott's health club during a layover in Chicago. He went on to win the Big Ten title and two weeks later won the national championship—one of three NCAA titles he would win during his great career.

This story is an example of how good communication can overcome problems. Barry respected the team enough to communicate the problem through a note. His teammates, roommates, and even the security officers helped the search for Barry by communicating important information. Most importantly, once I found Barry the good communication that we had developed before the incident made it possible for us to overcome the problem. A brief talk and a good workout was all it took to avert what might have been a devastating blow to a young man's athletic career. If you develop good lines of communication with your wrestlers, then you will be able to resolve problems to your and your wrestlers' benefit.

COMMUNICATING WITH ASSISTANT COACHES

Assistant coaches are very valuable to a wrestling program, if the head coach consults them and gives them the necessary authority. Assistants are good checkpoints who can confirm or raise questions about the approach the head coach is taking. If the head coach doesn't consult his assistants, then the coach defeats the purpose for having them. A head coach has too many responsibilities to do everything well. When capable help is available, it is a shame to shortchange the wrestlers in your program.

Good communication will get everyone involved and enthused about their roles. At every wrestling practice, the coaching staff must be on the same page. Otherwise, your wrestlers will be getting a set of instructions from one coach and a different set of instructions from another coach. That's not good. Throughout each practice, the head coach makes adjustments based on the wrestlers' performance. Assistants should be asked for their input and support for such decisions. Not only will this make for a better practice, but it will also keep the whole coaching staff interested in the program.

The whole staff needs to be working in similar directions for maximum gains. Seated from left to right are Jim Zalesky, Tom Brands, Royce Alger, and Dan Gable.

COMMUNICATING WITH THE ADMINISTRATION

Establishing a good relationship with administrators is important for any coach. If you can make the administration believe in you, then you can go about your business without constantly looking over your shoulder. If you need something, you'll find that administrators are much more likely to fulfill your request if you have developed good relations with them.

Coaches who have ongoing battles with the athletic director, principal, dean, and other members of the administration need to realize that the chain of command is necessary in any business, organization, or school. It's not about power; it's about efficient decision-making and division of labor. You want the administration to work with you, not against you, so don't try to undermine it. Keep surprises to a minimum, especially unpleasant ones. Administrators will respect and trust you if you treat them with respect and behave in a trustworthy manner.

A Little Wood Does Some Good

Every fall the wrestlers split wood in a forested area near Iowa City, owned by Bob Altmaier, a good wrestling supporter. Wood chopping is a great workout. Plus, afterwards, we give the extra wood to individuals who are important to the wrestling program. One person who almost always receives a load of wood is the athletic director. The athletes know that it helps to have the director on their side, and it's their way of showing some appreciation for supporting their sport.

Show the administration that your interest in your athletes goes beyond their wrestling performance. If you emphasize academics and proper conduct, that will be reflected by everyone in your program and will surely get administrators' attention. I disagree with the way the coaching staff is discouraged from communicating with faculty at most

Working closely with your athletic director (Bob Bowlsby, left) and your school president (Hunter Rawlings, right) can be very beneficial.

universities, especially because it is the coach who is usually held accountable for athletes' academic problems. If the faculty and coach communicate directly, the coach can demonstrate to them how supportive he is of their efforts to educate the student-athletes. If your school limits coach-faculty communication, abide by the ground rules and do the best you can under the circumstances. Administrators want to eliminate questionable perceptions, which is the main reason for restricting coach-faculty communication.

The administration has the right to expect you to comply with rules. Do so. Don't try to look for that tiny edge that might be gained by holding an extra, illegal practice session, and stay clear of recruiting infractions. Simply get more accomplished within the frame of the rules. If you have any doubt about a rule, check with the athletic director or another administrator who is responsible for having that information. By following the spirit and the letter of the rules, you'll enhance your relationship with the administration.

Staying current on NCAA legislation and rules helps you avoid unwanted predicaments.

COMMUNICATING WITH THE MEDIA

Wrestling has not fully utilized the media. We coaches must do more to promote our great sport. I don't mean designing glitzy media packages or doing something bizarre to get attention. Instead, I mean working at it through effective and tireless communication. You have to make covering your program convenient and pleasurable. Here are just a few of the ways:

- Arrange media days before and during the season.
- Send each nearby media outlet a schedule with a personal note inviting them to attend your events.
- Be accessible as much as possible.
- Try to schedule media gatherings at times that do not conflict with other major sports events.
- Have refreshments handy for individuals covering your events.
- Provide neat and complete results and information to media at your competitions.
- Phone in the results of your matches to local news outlets that did not cover the match.

Encourage the members of the media to contact you directly, but don't wait for them to come to you. Phone in stories and results related to competitions. You might also point out to the media certain "human interest" stories involving members of your team. Make sure that the kids get the ink, not the coaching staff.

Some reporters don't bother to cover wrestling because they don't know much about the sport. Take time to educate them. Spend an hour before the season with key media sources and give them a quick lesson on wrestling basics, particularly the scoring system. It's amazing how much more they appreciate wrestling when they learn what it is. Have them come to a few practices to give them a feel for the sport and its athletes and coaches. The more they know, the more they'll respect, and probably like, the sport.

Stories Worthy of Attention

Wrestling has hundreds of great human interest stories that should be told, and it's a coach's responsibility to bring these to the attention of the media. Some of the best wrestlers I've known and coached were just one of many children in homes where sharing was required, luxuries were few, and individual initiative was an imperative. For example, the outstanding Banach brothers, Ed and Lou, came from a large foster family. More recently, Lee Fullhart was raised in a very big family that included many adopted children, along with several other paternal children.

Great times can happen in families that pull together no matter what the circumstances are. Mr. and Mrs. Alan Tooley brought these three Banachs—Ed, Steve, and Lou—into their home and raised them well.

COMMUNICATING WITH FANS

Booster and support groups are important to the success of any wrestling program. Wrestlers' parents, students and their parents, community members, and other wrestling enthusiasts will back your program, if you give them a reason to. Take time to develop relationships with key people who can serve as leaders of support groups.

For example, after every home meet I speak to a select group at a social gathering. During that time, I give them special insight and reactions to the competition. Instead of having to read my responses in the paper the next day, these supporters get to hear it that night directly from the source. This gesture solidifies the support that this important group of people gives to the program. Therefore, they are more enthusiastic about getting others to back the team.

The student body is a very special support group. If you capture this group's spirit and energy, the administration will never overlook the importance of your program. With all of the distractions and attractions available to kids today, however, getting students to attend meets is not easy. You might ask assistant coaches for help in working with leaders of the student body. Together they can come up with some creative ideas for drawing more students to your events. Take time to attend student functions and talk with students in the hallway, cafeteria, dorm, or other places where they gather. If possible, enlist the team captains to help you emphasize the importance of student support of the program.

COMMUNICATING WITH THE WRESTLING COMMUNITY

Because of all the work you have to do with your own program, it's easy to put on the blinders and miss what is going on in the world beyond your wrestling room. Don't let that happen. Wrestling coaches and state and national wrestling organizations have much information to share. Make time to network with these individuals and groups—they can provide valuable insight and support.

Also, stay in touch with the sport's national governing body, USA Wrestling. It has a coaching education program that can benefit your professional development and provide opportunities to coach teams in regional, national, and international events.

SUMMARY

Effective communication is essential to being a successful wrestling coach. These are the key points to keep in mind:

- Show genuine interest in and respect for your athletes.
- Be true to your personality.
- Practice what you preach.
- Be a leader but always look to develop leaders on your team.
- Encourage the input of assistant coaches; it can be invaluable.
- Keep administrators informed and convey your respect for them and the rules.
- Don't wait for the media to come to you; promote your program and make it easy and fun for reporters to cover your events.
- Make the necessary contacts to get student and booster support.
- Keep in touch with the larger wrestling world through talks with other coaches, conventions, publications, and educational programs.

Chapter 3

MOTIVATING WRESTLERS

He's a taskmaster, but many of the USA's top prospects come to Iowa City, where they warm themselves against Gable's competitive fires, which still burn brightly . . . To a man, the Hawkeyes mirror Gable's take-no-prisoners approach. They attack for seven minutes, fighting through fatigue the way Gable did.—**USA Today, *February 1992***

Motivation is the driving force behind great achievements in wrestling, sports, academics, professional careers, or any pursuit where work is required. Motivation is often the deciding factor in matches between two equally skilled opponents. Given a choice, all coaches would take the athlete who has the self-motivation to do off-season workouts, show up ready for practice every day, work tirelessly on improving his technique until he's mastered it, and squeeze out every ounce of his talent. Those kind of wrestlers are rare. More common are the kids who want to win badly but lack the drive to do what's necessary to develop the skills and conditioning that's required to win on a consistent basis. They're motivated more by external factors, such as awards and media attention, than they are by their own inner drive to excel.

A coach can play a very important role in the motivation of his wrestlers. Your enthusiasm for wrestling will rub off on them, even if they aren't as committed as you are to the sport. The wrestling bug is contagious. But maybe you are highly motivated and still have trouble getting your athletes to the proper level of motivation. You might be reading this chapter in the hopes that I can give you some magical motivational method to use with your team. Sorry to disappoint you, but there's no magic formula when it comes to motivation. If there were and I knew exactly how to apply it, I wouldn't have had problems motivating certain individuals and teams during my coaching career.

Short on Motivation

Mark Reiland was an excellent wrestler in Iowa's program. As a junior in 1991, he was an NCAA champion at 167. But something was missing in '92. He got off to a slow start, but he had done that in previous years, so I didn't pay a lot of attention to it. Around midseason, it became obvious that what I had thought was an early-season slump was instead a total lack of motivation. Mark had seemingly lost his desire to compete, and it began looking like he might cut short his wrestling career.

I had missed all of the warning signs, which I would have seen if I had been more keyed into Mark's situation. Here was an athlete who at 20 years of age felt as though he had accomplished as much as he ever could in wrestling—winning the national title in front of the home fans the year before. Anything after that was anticlimactic, he felt. I failed to recognize that until it was too late. Mark was the only wrestler on the '92 team who did not make All-American.

If we had acted on early warning signs of a lack of motivation, Iowa's program would have had a record-setting 10 All-Americans in 1992. Returning NCAA champion, Mark Reiland struggled here with more than his opponent.

The Mark Reiland story should convince you that no matter how much experience or knowledge you have as a wrestling coach, you must pay attention to the motivational level of each individual on your team. It should also convince you, as it did me, that you can never take motivation for granted.

MOTIVATIONAL LEADERSHIP

I've always thought of motivation as the energy source that sustains successful wrestling programs. That energy flows from the coach and through each athlete on the team. Making athletes excited about what they are doing and providing them opportunities to fulfill their wrestling ambitions is extremely rewarding. A coach enhances or diminishes the motivation of wrestlers depending on the type of leadership he provides.

The changes in personnel each year increase the challenge of team motivation. Over time, athletes in the program will emerge as motivational leaders to their teammates. When this happens, the attitude spreads throughout the team, and new leaders set the example each year.

THE MOTIVATION CHALLENGE

Staying motivated when you have success is relatively easy. Your wrestlers can see that the training and techniques you are teaching them are paying off, which motivates them to work harder. When you see that they are motivated, that in turn motivates you. But everyone can't always win, nor will performances always meet expectations. These situations can challenge an athlete's, and a coach's, motivation. In those cases, you and your athletes better have well-established sources of motivation you can rely on until the breaks start going your way.

Personal Motivation

Great motivators are themselves very highly motivated. Once you reach that high level of motivation, you need to maintain it to stay on top. If you lose it, regaining it may be difficult. My motivation for coaching has several sources. First, I love the sport. Wrestling excellence is the ultimate in individual and team achievement in athletics. It takes a complete commitment to attain it. Second, I love helping athletes seeking wrestling excellence to achieve it. The teaching, the motivation, the workouts, and all that goes into helping develop champions are what I enjoy doing.

Third, I love the wrestling competition. A clean, hard-fought wrestling match is the most honest of athletic contests. There are no technological interventions, no teammates to blame, no panel of judges to bias the score. In wrestling, you compete or you quit. No ali-

bis—I like that. The final source of my motivation, one that I think most top wrestlers and coaches share, is a desire for greatness. This necessary inner force is required to become a legend in our sport. My own drives, as a wrestler and a coach, allowed me to achieve what others have not.

Athlete Motivation

Now that I've put all the emphasis on the coach's motivation, let me say that no one can motivate a wrestler who does not like the sport, is not receptive to teaching, and has no desire to compete. It's impossible. Hopefully, all your wrestlers will at least begin their careers with great enthusiasm. The great wrestling programs have athletes who are supercommitted; these wrestlers don't stay down when things go poorly. Because of their positive mindset, they are capable of incredible athletic feats.

A whole team of supercommitted individuals is rare, however. Some wrestlers just never seem to reach the high level of motivation necessary to be champions. Some have social, academic, or athletic interests that take away from their wrestling motivation. Still others who were once motivated—perhaps even champions at one time—lose their motivation for the sport.

You and I face these motivational challenges every year. It's impossible for me to prescribe any motivational technique that is sure to work in every case. If I had one, I would have used it with Mark Reiland and other athletes I've coached. On the other hand, I do have some suggestions for you. Try some of the following techniques that have helped motivate myself and my wrestlers. You probably use some of them already.

Talking One-on-One

The easiest and most basic motivational approach is to meet with each of your wrestlers individually and to do so frequently. Don't just wait until something bad happens. If you can't always arrange face-to-face talks, call them on the phone. Listen to them. Make sure that

Leading Brands

The start of the '92 season was filled with high expectations. None of the starters from the '91 NCAA Championship team had graduated yet. All except one had been All-American. Another title was a lock—at least according to the "experts." Yet I was fearful that the team might grow complacent and underachieve, so I did something to prevent that from happening. I went to my most credentialed wrestler, Tom Brands, a three-time All-American and two-time NCAA champion, and asked him to take the lead. I told him that he was the example that the rest of the team would look to in terms of performance and confidence.

The big risk in doing this was if Tom faltered or was seriously injured, the rest of the team might collapse. Yet I felt that there was less chance of that happening than there was that the team would not reach its potential without a team leader. Tom accepted the leadership role and the team followed him right to another NCAA Championship. Furthermore, Tom's example gave the underclassmen a model to follow in future years as they take the leadership role.

Look to your most experienced and credentialed athlete to help bring the team to its potential. Tom Brands fit this description for the 1992 season.

they know you have a special care for them as people. Just letting your athletes share with you the many things affecting them can be a tremendous boost to their motivation. By listening to them, you also might be able to help them achieve the things that are important to them. They'll appreciate it.

Setting Goals

Motivation is closely related to establishing, monitoring, and adjusting goals. In your one-on-one and team meetings with your wrestlers, help them set goals that are measurable, challenging but realistic, performance-based, specific, and important to them and the program. Include subgoals that will serve as motivators toward the big goals. Don't just limit the goals to wrestling; also address academic objectives and identify desirable social behaviors for athletes. Then, as they meet or come close to the targets, look for ways to broaden or extend your wrestlers' goals. Through this process, athletes and teams not only improve their level of achievement, they also have a performance standard that is independent of the competition. That standard is crucial for achieving consistency and excellence.

Experiencing Fun and Success

As important as a positive relationship with and proper direction from a coach are to an athlete, personal talks and goals aren't enough for many wrestlers. They need to enjoy the sport and realize some degree of success on the mat. How you design and conduct practices (see chapter 6) has a lot to do with how much fun and success they experience and therefore how motivated they are. This is especially true for reserve wrestlers, but it also applies to the stars on the team.

Success, when defined as getting the most out of your potential within a given situation, can be achieved by every athlete. Success produces a positive feeling that athletes want to experience again and again. As a result of success experiences, your wrestlers will give greater effort in order to achieve even greater success. The saying that "success breeds success" is true, as is the saying that "success and fun breed motivation."

Publicizing for Motivation

Everyone likes to have their accomplishments recognized. I'm sure your wrestlers and your coaching staff (not to mention you and me) get a little more pumped up when they get positive public recognition. Make sure it gets to the public. One very effective promotion that motivates Iowa wrestlers is the annual poster schedule. The design is attractive and meaningful for each season.

The athletes know that if they become All-Americans before their senior year they will appear on the poster. This fact motivates them to excel as undergraduates and gives the seniors the recognition they deserve. Even the fans look forward to each year's poster; they appreciate the design and look for a clue to that season's mission. Some fans even frame the posters and save them as collector's items.

The following are four posters from the past with a brief commentary about their meaning and the people shown.

The 1985 poster was a take-off of the television show *Dallas,* which was extremely popular at the time. I'm emulating the show's lead character, J.R. Ewing, one of the most disliked TV personalities ever. Just as *Dallas* dominated the Nielsens, Iowa's wrestling team dominated NCAA wrestling. We were seven-time defending champion going into this season, and people outside of our program liked us about as much as they liked J.R. Everyone wanted to stop us from getting our eighth consecutive title. Very simply, it was the United States vs. Iowa. We wanted our wrestlers and fans to know that and to be prepared for the challenges we would face. The All-Americans shown on the poster are (from left to right) Lindley Kistler, Barry Davis, Jim Heffernan, Duane Goldman, Greg Randall, and Marty Kistler.

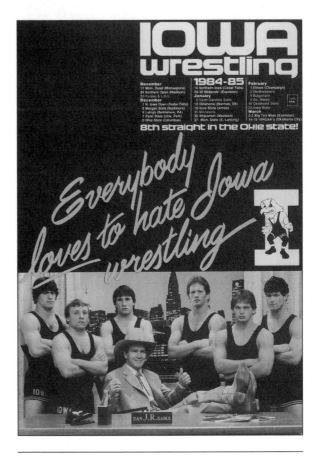

1985 poster

The Roman numeral for 10, X, was on the mind of everyone in 1987. X represented our quest for a tenth straight NCAA Championship, which at that time would set an all-time record for consecutive titles for any NCAA sport. That season was all about making history. X was everywhere—on our uniforms, on sweatshirts, on bumper stickers, you name it. I guess we were too swept up in the whole thing and too confident for we came up short of that tenth straight NCAA title. From left to right, the people are Rico Chiapparelli, Greg Randall, Jim Heffernan, Brad Penrith, Royce Alger, and me.

1987 poster

The team had ended its nine-year reign as NCAA champs, so I felt it needed to refocus its priorities. Although my previous approach had been very successful, the title loss gave me courage to change some things that had been bothering me about the program. The 1988 poster reflects the new emphasis of the program: academics, clean living, and all of

the other values that are crucial to being a true champion.

In the poster, Professor Gable is introducing the "new school" of Iowa wrestling and tossing out the "old school," which is symbolized by bad press (newspapers), excessive and poor social behaviors (empty cans), and counting championships before they were won (uniform with X on it). This season was the turning point—a breath of fresh air and great motivation for our program. The All-Americans from left to right are Brad Penrith, John Heffernan, Mark Sindlinger, and Royce Alger.

On the 1997 poster I'm checking the list to see which former All-American or NCAA champion has a chance to win or repeat. The "To Be Determined" wrestler represents anyone else on the squad who wants to step up to this category. Ironically, the "To Be Determined" is Jessie Whitmer who ended up being an NCAA champion that year. At the time, Jessie wasn't a starter.

Iowa has been printing poster schedules since 1980. Even if you can't afford an expen-

1988 poster

1997 poster

sive color annual poster, I highly recommend doing something like this. You'll find that it's a great motivational tool. Publicity efforts beyond an annual poster also help. Hold a media day before your first competition each year to give your wrestlers some publicity. Not only is this experience a good motivator, but it can also help your athletes become more skillful and articulate in responding to the media.

Your own statements transmitted through newspaper, radio, and television outlets can also serve as motivators. Mostly, take the positive approach without putting too much pressure on the team or any individual wrestler. If you have good kids and respect the things that should be kept between you and them, they'll get inspired by watching or reading your comments about them.

Choosing Team Leaders

The selection of team captains can be detrimental or positive to the motivation of team members, depending on how you handle it.

Force an unpopular or weak wrestler into the position, and it can spell disaster. Get respected and strong individuals into the role of captains, and you have a tremendous additional source of motivation on your team.

I wait until the team has practiced three or four weeks before determining the captains. By waiting at least a few weeks before selecting captains, you can avoid errors and confirm that the choices you have in mind are best for the team and the individuals you pick. Sometimes, in addition to the obvious choice, I also select a not-so-obvious wrestler who may benefit as a person and wrestler from being placed in a leadership position.

Setting Up a Motivational Environment

I'm a big believer that the work environment has a big impact on performance. Be it the study areas for schoolwork or the training areas for wrestling, the setting should motivate the student or athlete to focus and excel. At this point, some of you may be saying "I don't have the financial support to create a great wrestling room." To that I reply, "Make the best of what you have, and always look for ways to improve it." Even if you have the most spartan of workout facilities, keep it clean and well-organized. You must make the area and equipment conducive to training, especially in regard to health and safety standards.

The Iowa wrestling team is fortunate to have a state-of-the-art wrestling facility for training (see figure 3.1 on page 32). Notice the layout of the weights, mats, ropes, and so forth. All are quickly accessible, but no workout area intrudes on the space of another area. The walls are painted with school colors and filled with special phrases that recruits, athletes, and coaches find motivating.

An inspiring workout facility is important, but you shouldn't stop there. Also strive to make the sites of your team's competitions motivating to your wrestlers. The best way is to have your fans pack the house at each event. A facility full of supporters rooting your wrestlers on in each match will help bring out the maximum potential of your athletes and will give them something to look forward to while preparing for every competition.

Steiner Plus Three

Troy Steiner was the obvious pick for captain of the 1992–93 team. Troy was a great leader, highly dedicated, and the only returning NCAA champion on the team. However, Troy's twin brother Terry, a two-time All-American and just as dedicated, also deserved consideration. The two other senior All-Americans were deserving as well, and I thought they might benefit from the leadership responsibility. After four weeks, I decided that Troy would be the lead captain and do all the talking and decision-making associated with that role. The other three seniors would serve as co-captains and lead through their examples in wrestling practices, academics, and social activities.

Troy, as head of the captains, demonstrated his leadership and willingness to sacrifice himself to strengthen the team by making room for Lincoln McIlravy at his weight class. Troy then went on to win a big match at the Big Ten meet to defeat Penn State's last chance to knock us off. At the NCAA championships, Troy came through to score valuable team points in wrestle-backs after a tough loss earlier in the competition.

Having deep meaning within a team will help individuals make extra sacrifices to help out. Troy Steiner is just one important example of this valued concept.

Imagining for Motivation

As a kid, I always dreamed of future success. Some of the dreams were fantasies, such as outperforming Jim Brown on the football field or outslugging Mickey Mantle in Yankee Stadium. In one memorable dream, I imagined myself wrestling the legend Frank Gotch for the World Championship with thousands of fans providing a carnival-type atmosphere for the match. Inspiring and pleasant thoughts, but not too practical.

As I developed into a competitive athlete, I began using my imagination for more real-life events. I'd visualize my performance in future matches against likely opponents, seeing them attempt to counter my moves, as well as giving in to a relentless attack. With success, I began to visualize myself competing in future Olympic Games. Throughout my wrestling and coaching, I have continued this use of imagery.

Athletes and coaches must visualize greatness to achieve it. Well before competitions, wrestlers and wrestling coaches must see themselves performing positively in their upcoming events. Imagery is a great source of motivation, and it can be very helpful in learning and refining certain wrestling techniques and tactics. If done correctly, imagery is similar to "live" drilling on the mat, where wrestlers feel, see, smell, and hear themselves performing perfectly. I'll discuss this concept further in part III.

Using Additional Motivational Tools

Wrestling publications are a great source of motivation. The more informed about and involved in the sport your wrestlers are, the more they'll want to achieve. *Wrestling USA* emphasizes high school wrestling. *Amateur Wrestling News* and *W.I.N.* focus on the college level. *USA Wrestler* centers around freestyle and Greco wrestling. In addition, several states have their own wrestling publications, typically covering all levels of competition. Iowa has the *Predicament*. Illinois has *The Grappler*. Wisconsin publishes *Crossface*, and Pennsylvania puts out the *Roundup*. Check the appendix for a listing of wrestling publications and their addresses.

Videotapes can also serve to motivate wrestlers. Watching themselves perform can make them more positive about their abilities and inspire them to work harder. Watching other great wrestlers can drive them to achieve a higher level of performance. At Iowa, many inspirational books and files full of inspirational stories and motivational sayings are available for the wrestlers to read. (*The Heart of a Champion* by Bob Richards should be required reading for every wrestler who wants to achieve something.)

An entire wall of the Iowa wrestling office complex shows photos of all the NCAA champions from our program. Another wall is filled with names of all of Iowa's previous All-Americans and Big Ten champions. Impressive trophy cases contain much of the hardware Iowa's championship teams have earned. Finally, awards that recognize each year's most valuable wrestler, the graduating senior letter winner with the highest grade point average, the most courageous wrestler, and the wrestler that is most distinguished off the mat as well as on it are also posted. These awards are actually named after special people that have been associated with Iowa wrestling over the years. The most valuable was in memory of Mike Howard, Iowa's first wrestling coach. The most courageous is in memory of Michael J. McGivern, Sr. who passed away in the stands of a Midlands Wrestling tournament while his son, Mike Jr., was in the event. The academic award is in memory of J. Donald McPike, whose sons, Richard and Don, still follow the Hawks closely each season. The last annual award, given to the wrestler that has unique characteristics off the mat as well, is in memory of John H. Sill. John never missed any action, on or off the mat—his camera's pictures proved so. Besides solving the decorating problem in the office area, these photos, trophies, and awards give the athletes something to strive for as individuals and as a team. They provide a great deal of support for the athletes and families involved and can inspire your team too.

SUMMARY

You probably already use many of the motivational approaches I've cited. This was only a small sample; we all have special ways of motivating certain individuals in certain situations. If you take just one thing from this chapter, it should be this: the motivation of everyone in your program reflects your own motivation. You are the primary source of motivation. If your motivation drops, the athletes and fans who might need a boost aren't likely to be fully motivated. Talking one-on-one, setting goals, providing fun and success, using positive imagery, choosing good team captains, getting publicity for individuals and the team, creating a great environment, and all the other motivators mentioned in this chapter will help only if you have the personal motivation to implement them. Be the motivating leader that your athletes deserve.

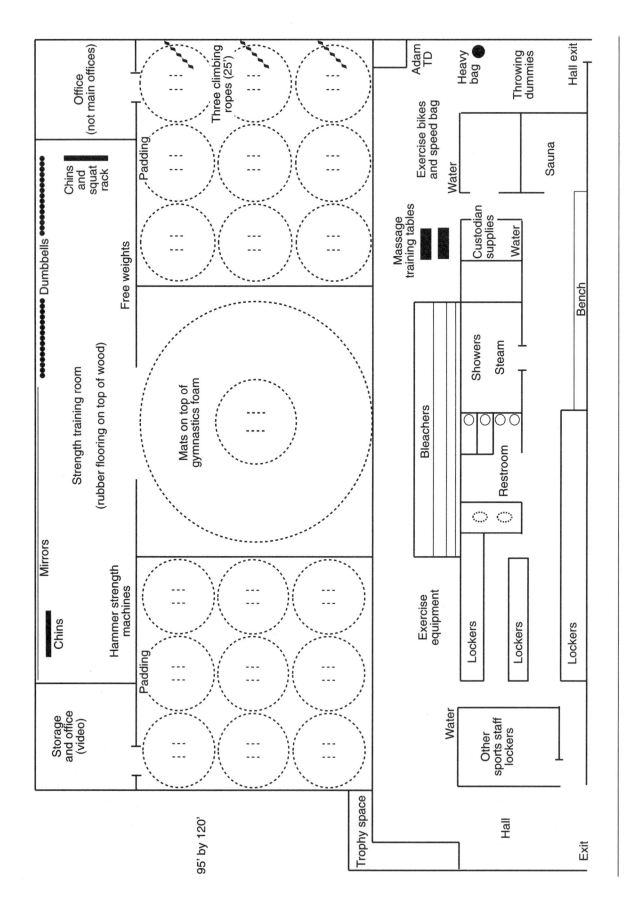

Figure 3.1 Iowa's wrestling facilities

Chapter
4

BUILDING A CHAMPIONSHIP WRESTLING PROGRAM

Everyone is looking for the perfect program. Coaches want to build it, wrestlers want to be part of it, and fans want to identify with it. Only one problem: there's no such thing. Even the University of Iowa and other colleges, high schools, and clubs that have established highly successful wrestling programs have flaws. What separates the top programs from the rest of the pack is that they have fewer weaknesses, and the weaknesses they have are in less important areas. When they do find a problem, they normally correct it quickly and decisively. They keep moving ahead.

Although I can't help you build the perfect program, I can share with you the approach that I've had success with at Iowa. Woven through this approach are many of the valuable lessons I learned while wrestling in great programs in high school under Coach Bob Siddens and in college under Dr. Harold Nichols and at the start of my coaching career under Iowa Head Coach Gary Kurdelmeier. All of these experiences and lessons helped me develop what's proven to be a formula for success.

Gary Kurdelmeier, in addition to being the great architect in starting Iowa's wrestling program on its dominant ways, was also a great wrestler himself. Gary won an NCAA championship at Iowa after starring at famous Cresco High School, home of many great names like Nichols, Peckham, Flannigan, and Bourlag.

THE FOUNDATION

Before I get into what it takes to build and maintain a top wrestling program, remember that all of this information won't mean much if you, personally, haven't addressed the areas covered in the first three chapters. Take stock of yourself:

✓ Examine your philosophy. Is your outlook positive? Do your athletes come first?

✓ Consider how you communicate with your athletes and others around your wrestling program. Are you an effective leader and listener?

✓ Make an honest assessment of your own motivation and your ability to motivate others. Do you have the enthusiasm that's necessary to put in the extra hours and inspire your wrestlers to reach their potential?

If you're struggling in one of these fundamental areas, you'll have trouble building and maintaining a championship program. Even if you have all of the other things—big budget, great athletes, superior facilities—going for you, your program's foundation will be weak and will eventually crumble. You might win for a year or two, but then it will fall apart.

You don't have to look too far to find programs where this has happened. Even after several years of success at Iowa, the program was susceptible to a steep drop when the team let little problems go until they became big problems. The team had to re-evaluate and re-establish its priorities before it could turn things around and return to a top level. So even if you're on top now, check your program's foundation to make sure you're on solid ground.

Building Block #1: Athletes

Although the leader of the program must have his act together, no wrestling coach has won a title by himself. You can't go out on the mat and wrestle. You have to accept the fact that your fate is in the hands of your athletes.

That's why the quality and quantity of athletes you have in your program is a major factor in determining your success.

It's no accident that the dominant wrestling programs typically have at least two or three great wrestlers on their team each year. The program must breed those kinds of athletes to maintain its level. To do so, you must attract sufficient numbers to the team. A certain percentage of kids, although they want to be the best, are going to find it extremely difficult to ever gain the top spot. The more wrestlers you have, the bigger the talent pool and the more likely it is that you'll have a strong athlete at each weight.

If you're coaching at the high school level, you need to make sure that you stay in touch with the junior high, middle, and elementary school youngsters in your area. Get them into your summer camps. Teach them the techniques that you emphasize in your program. Encourage them to wrestle with a local age-group team or on their own in the many competitions available for young, developing wrestlers. These kids are your future.

Work with local coaches at all levels to develop good relations and to make sure that the wrestlers are being taught consistently and correctly. Invite the coaches to attend your practices. If you have a chance, go see a practice or match involving each of the coaches' teams. They'll appreciate your interest, and it will mean even more to the kids who are wrestling in their programs. Often, young wrestlers learn beginning techniques from coaches who are volunteering their time and may not know the most up-to-date techniques. In these cases, less updated skills could result in fewer great wrestlers down the road, especially if some of these techniques result in bad habits that are hard to change. Young people need to learn good skills from the beginning to help eliminate the forming of bad technical habits. Your job will be a lot easier if athletes have learned good wrestling from the start.

If you're a club coach or college coach, then the talent pool you have is determined by your ability and resources to recruit. That doesn't mean you're stuck if somebody else gets more gifted athletes. You can still outwork and outcoach them, but you must recruit sufficient numbers and talent to get the job done. From personal experience, I know that my job is much easier if I bring in a solid group of student-athletes to the university each year.

Assuming you have a sizable pool of athletes from which to draw your talent each year and that they have learned the basic wrestling skills, your next step is to instill in them the dedication and desire it takes to be a champion. Oftentimes, it takes two or three wrestlers who have a positive attitude to provide the example for the rest of the team. Leaders have a tremendous, positive effect during the season and off-season. Their attitude, work habits, and lifestyle provide the model for their peers and the younger, aspiring wrestlers in the community. Once you have the athletes, and they have the attitudes of champions, then your ability to train and teach them is most important. I'll cover those areas in subsequent chapters.

Extra A.M. Work

Coach Siddens always encouraged the West Waterloo High wrestlers to come into school for a 6:30 A.M. training session. He figured that this additional work could mean the difference in a tight match. The workout he recommended consisted of 15 to 20 minutes of running in the gym, followed by sprints, rope skipping, chin-ups, and push-ups. Coach Siddens didn't require this extra early morning work, but he emphasized it more and more throughout the season and especially before tournament time.

Doug Moses, a teammate and close friend who now coaches wrestling at the University of Southern Colorado, and I began doing the before-school workouts from day one. The other members of the team figured they would wait for tourney time before they began doing the extra work. But after Doug and I wrestled so well in early season matches, we soon had company at our morning practice sessions. As a result, the team's performance improved noticeably, and its season was that much more successful.

Building Block #2: Facilities and Equipment

Some aspects of building a program present the chicken-and-egg dilemma. For example, do great facilities draw great wrestlers, or do great wrestlers provide the funds and interest in building great facilities? Whatever the case, you need a safe, clean, and motivating environment to be highly successful. You don't need a penthouse, but you need something better than an outhouse. Most coaches are in a position where they have to make the best use of what's available. Practice facilities don't have to be perfect, just safe and clean. After the program achieves some success, you should be able to make a convincing argument for upgrading what you have.

If you're fortunate enough to have good facilities and equipment, make it available to your athletes. A locked-up facility does no one any good. I see to it that all of the facilities and equipment are available throughout the year to the wrestlers, practically around the clock each day. My challenge to them is to wear out the equipment through use, not abuse, so it has to be replaced.

Of course, liability is a big concern for all of us. You can't watch the facilities 24 hours a day to make sure that nothing happens, so you need to arrange for supervision when your facility is open. It may cost the program a bit of money, but it is a wise investment. Oftentimes, responsible volunteers, such as parents, assistant coaches, or former wrestlers, will be willing to help out and ease the financial burden.

If local school or community facilities are not available, you may have to find other options. When I was student-teaching in Humboldt, Iowa, I took advantage of the local police station's weight room, which was open 24 hours a day. Perhaps a wrestler will have a set of weights and a workout area in his home and might be willing to have teammates over for workouts. Whatever the case, the development of wrestlers and a wrestling program requires adequate facilities and equipment. When you do have these things, make them accessible to maximize their benefit for the athletes on your team.

Building Block #3: Support Staff

The importance of quality personnel in the program doesn't stop with the head coach and athletes. Assistant coaches, managers, trainers, statisticians, and everyone else involved play a role in your success. Treat these individuals with great respect, as you want them to treat you. Define their responsibilities very clearly when they start, evaluate and communicate with them regularly, and adjust their duties if it is in the program's benefit to do so. In my 25 years with University of Iowa wrestling, two people have been consistently in charge of the wrestling office. My personal thanks to Helen Hohle and, more recently, to Judy Leonard. Good office help is a must.

Building Block #4: Administration, Student, Parent, and Community Support

A wrestling program doesn't exist on its own. Although wrestling receives little attention because of misconceptions and the priority given other sports, I've never understood why many wrestling coaches do very little to generate more support from those outside the program. Even if your team is not having great success, you may have an individual or two who is deserving of attention. Perhaps an athlete has a special story that will generate interest and goodwill toward the program.

Good copy will only go so far. The program, or at least individuals within the program, must be successful on the mat if you are going to gain and sustain the support of the administration, student body, wrestlers' parents, and community members. In addition, you must provide personal attention to these four groups. That takes a little time, but it's well worth it. A few phone calls each day, a speech or two each week, and occasional meetings will pay big dividends.

The Bump Elliott Rule

Right after I came to coach at the University of Iowa, I had a meeting with Bump Elliott, who was the athletic director. I'll never forget what Bump said to me: "Don't ask for the moon. Strive to get there, sure, but do it wisely through continuing to build upon what you already have. As you build, come see me, and we'll see how I can help out." I now call that bit of wisdom the Bump Elliott Rule, and it serves as a good reminder to keep things in perspective. Gradual, solid growth is better than any shaky quick fix.

My only request that first year was for new wrestling mats for the athletes. The old mats were in bad shape and unsafe, hindering their training. Just this simple change motivated the wrestlers, who didn't expect anyone cared enough to ask for or get better equipment for them.

The next year, after winning the school's first conference championship in 12 seasons, I requested minor improvements for the locker room. The old, beat-up, closed lockers were replaced with new, open locker areas; the revamped shower area had new wall and floor tiles and shower heads and disinfectant soap dispensers; and a sauna was added, which offered many benefits to our overall training. (Saunas and steam rooms are illegal in high school settings. Unfortunately, these facilities have been abused in the past by programs looking for a quick method of weight cutting.) All of these items enhanced the health, hygiene, and atmosphere for the athletes' training. The benefits of the new mats and upgraded locker facilities were realized quickly. The attitude and performance of the team improved considerably, and recruiting efforts were helped tremendously.

Being successful is always easier if your boss is willing to work with you rather than against you. I always wanted to do good things and a lot had to do with the athletic director that recruited me to Iowa—Bump Elliott.

Iowa has several groups in the local community that bring attention to the wrestling program. Kids' wrestling clubs in the area get youngsters and their families involved in the sport and generate interest and fan support for us. The same is true of the school programs in and near Iowa City. We also have a local sports club called the Hawkeye Wrestling Club that promotes wrestling statewide and nationally. Several Olympians have wrestled for this club, which serves to bring further attention to the success that Iowa's program has had.

A fan group called H.A.W.K., short for Hawkeye Area Wrestling Klub, is a big source of support. H.A.W.K. was organized by local wrestling enthusiasts, and this group provides a solid fan base. In addition, the group

A Special Helper

In the late '70s, Iowa had a wrestling manager, Brett Mangold, who did such an exceptional job that I was able to convince the university to hire him after his graduation, first on a part-time basis and then as a full-time aid. Brett was able to provide administrative assistance to the coaching staff in many areas, including travel plans and financial matters. Brett also put together Iowa's video library, which would not have been nearly as complete or organized if left to me or the coaching staff to develop.

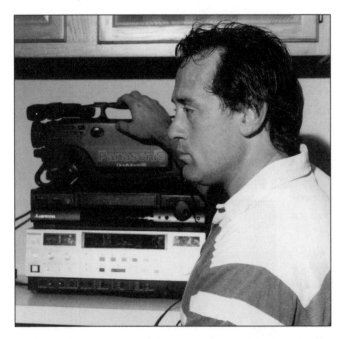

Brett Mangold has put together a library of wrestling tapes over many years. This library has aided Iowa's program immensely.

sets up special social functions in conjunction with Iowa's wrestling events. A special fan support group can add a great deal to a program, so show your appreciation for these key supporters. Three individuals who've been instrumental in organizing Iowa's fan support better than anywhere else in the country are Bob Dane, Morrie Adams, and Ed McGinness. In addition, Tom Senneff and Ron Rogers have been on the local wrestling club's board of directors since its founding in 1973. A program can thrive with this kind of loyalty and commitment from fans.

Building Block #5: Off-Season Work

There's no substitute for good, hard work. Show me a successful wrestling program, and I'll show you a coach and a group of wrestlers who work to improve themselves during the off-season. As a coach, I want to do all I can to improve my teaching of skills and tactics and to increase my knowledge of training methods and nutrition. I'll also want to work some camps and communicate with other coaches to perhaps add something beneficial to my program. As for the athletes, having one or two reliable wrestlers who can be positive examples in the off-season for others to follow is important to the improvement of the program from one year to the next. Strength training, running, and wrestling workouts are the most beneficial components of off-season training. Of course getting freestyle or Greco-Roman training and competitions during the off-season is very beneficial, but a wrestler's success in academics will determine just how much off-season training can be put in.

Summer Camps

I'm an advocate of summer wrestling camps; wrestlers and coaches can gain a great deal from them. You're bound to learn something about technique and training that will help you during the next season, and probably for the rest of your career. Plus, the competition and social opportunities afforded in these camps are invaluable to the maturation of a developing wrestler.

At the same time, I'm a firm believer in not pushing someone too fast. I've seen too many wrestlers burn out early or develop mental blocks about competition. Some wrestlers learn to accept losing to older and more advanced wrestlers, and then fail to get motivated for matches against peers in their own age category. When young athletes are ready to go to camp or compete at a higher level, it should be apparent. Don't force them.

Here are my recommendations for camps and clinics for specific age groups:

- **Elementary school.** For the most part, stick with local day camps offered by community clubs and youth sports programs. If such camps aren't available or the wrestler is

Twins Survive and Thrive

The Steiner twins, Troy and Terry, were highly successful wrestlers at Iowa, but the story of how they ever made it to a mat was even more remarkable. Born prematurely, they each weighed about two pounds at birth. Their chances of survival weren't great, yet they fought for their lives under the watchful eye and care of physicians and nurses. After six months, they were stable enough to be released from the hospital and go home—each in a shoe box. It is truly amazing that these two tiny infants would, through their own incredible dedication and sacrifice, become two of the best-conditioned athletes of all time.

The Steiner twins (Troy and Terry) made for great news copy. Terry is shown here.

advanced for his age, he might consider traveling to a stay-over youth wrestling camp. These youth camps should specialize in skill and activity work that is fun and simple. Ben and John Peterson, Olympic champions in 1972 and 1976, have a great father-son wrestling camp that enhances both knowledge of the sport and the relationship between the boy and his father.

- **Middle and junior high school.** This age group benefits most from technique camps that emphasize how to train to improve wrestling skills. Classroom topics at these camps should include proper attitude, strength and conditioning, and nutrition. It's also helpful if these young athletes are exposed to top-notch scholastic, collegiate, freestyle, and Greco-Roman wrestling at the camps, either in person or on videotape.

- **High school.** At this age, wrestlers are ready for more intensive training camps that emphasize technique. Some of the sessions can even have wrestlers working out at close to in-season intensity. Some camps pattern themselves after World or Olympic training camps, although the high school campers are shown more techniques. Advanced high school wrestlers might have the opportunity to participate in Olympic development or national camps, which provide great learning experiences for the athletes and expose them to college coaches who might be interested in recruiting them. Wrestling's national governing body, USA Wrestling, offers these types of camps in Colorado Springs. If you are interested, call 719-598-8181 for further information. The wrestling camps available at the University of Iowa offer both the advanced training camps and the shorter technical camps. For more information call 319-335-9714.

Stay informed of the most current rules on camps, off-season competitions, all-star events, and so on. The National Federation of State High School Associations, located in Kansas City, Missouri, administers to secondary school sports programs throughout the United States and can also be consulted, particularly for questions about rules (816-464-5400). Fi-

nally, your state high school athletic association is the first source you should contact if you have any questions on eligibility issues.

Advice to Wrestlers for the Off-Season

I would hesitate to tell student-athletes involved in wrestling what activities or sports they need to participate in. If a wrestler asks for guidance, however, I would tell him: "What you participate in is your decision. If you're interested in football, then I'd encourage you to try to play running back or linebacker. I've actually had success with athletes competing in two sports. Mark Sindlinger, two-time wrestling All-American, was also a starter on Iowa's football team. His scholarship was, of course, counted by football (a nice advantage). If you want to participate in baseball or track and field in the spring, then I strongly recommend adding a strength training program to the sport you choose. During the summer, try to find some time to attend wrestling camps and to do some freestyle and Greco-Roman wrestling, even if you're playing another sport. If nothing else, work hard at a summer job so that you're getting good exercise each day and keeping your body fit."

Building Block #6: Training Rules

Team and individual guidelines should be spelled out, along with the consequences that could result if those guidelines are violated. The athletic department should have a set of regulations that are standard for all athletes at the school. These rules are typically accompanied by predetermined consequences for violators.

In addition, you should have an additional set of guidelines specific to your team. Although your wrestlers should know what to expect if they break one of these team regulations, you should be flexible enough to adjust your penalties to best meet each situation. Suppose one of your wrestlers gets in trouble with the athletic department and is suspended from the next two competitions. That same violation may carry with it certain penalties according to the team's rules, such as extra

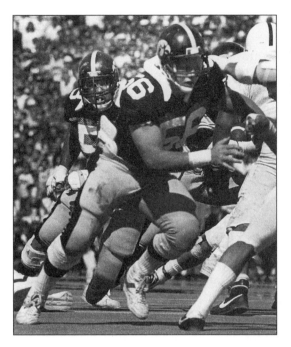 

Mark Sindlinger—two-time All-American—was an athlete that utilized his time schedule well. He played football and wrestled in college and did them both extremely well.

work during practice or additional responsibilities (such as cleaning the locker room or scrubbing the wrestling mats).

The Box

Iowa's practice facility has a penalty box where an athlete goes when certain things occur. Negligence in academics, such as cutting classes or missing appointments with professors and tutors, is the most common offense of the wrestlers that get put in the box. The box works on the same principle as the time-out method of disciplining children. By removing a wrestler from an activity that he wants to be part of, practice, I reduce the probability that the athlete will commit the same violation again. Plus, from a pride standpoint, it's very tough for an athlete to watch his teammates put in hard work and interact during practice and not be able to be part of it. I want all of my wrestlers to hate missing practice and therefore do all that they can to avoid being placed in the box.

Developing Responsible Athletes

I've covered a lot of territory in this chapter, and I've only hit upon the main points involved in building a wrestling program. There's one more thing that you can do to set your program above the rest, however. It's difficult to explain, but what it amounts to is teaching your athletes to stand on their own two feet and face the challenges they will face on the wrestling mat and in life.

Nurture in them a strong work ethic and discipline that will allow them to succeed. Put them in decision-making situations that require them to choose between right and wrong; the hard but rewarding way and the easy way out; the unselfish and selfish alternatives. Not only is this approach best for the individuals in your program, it's also a selling point to parents, school administrators, and community members who see the maturation of the wrestlers you work with. By asking athletes for more, you get more. My style of teaching isn't easy, as anyone who has seen one of my practices will agree, but the athletes thrive on the challenge. In this way, they become winners even before they step onto the mat.

SUMMARY

In this chapter, I've described the building blocks of a successful wrestling program. Remember that no matter how solid these blocks are, they'll crumble if you have failed to lay the proper coaching foundation in your own philosophy, communication, and motivation. Here are some of the main points:

- Surround yourself with great people, including athletes and support staff.

- Develop a feeder system that provides quality athletes with good technique and great attitude.

- Earn the respect of those you coach and work with and treat them with similar respect.

- Pinpoint leaders who will provide great examples for teammates, especially during the off-season.

- Strive to provide updated, clean, and accessible equipment and facilities for your athletes.

- Promote your program through booster clubs and the media.

- Familiarize yourself with the many summer wrestling camps available and encourage your athletes to participate in them.

- Stay in touch with local, state, and national organizations that govern wrestling rules and competitions.

- Develop a set of policies and consequences to prevent and address team and individual violations.

- Set your program apart by building champions who can succeed on and off the mat.

Part II

COACHING PLANS

Chapter

5

PLANNING FOR THE SEASON

Part I of this book focused on why we do what we do as coaches, including such important issues as our view of what's right and wrong, our choices as to whom we choose to communicate with and how, and the things that motivate us and our athletes. Our outlook on these things form the basis for how we approach each season. The rest of *Coaching Wrestling Successfully* centers around what I've done, and what you may want to do, as a coach. This part of the book examines the important planning process. Planning is a key element of any successful wrestling program. Good fortune is a product of good planning—there's no such thing as a lucky champion.

By planning, I'm talking about more than just deciding what you'll do the rest of the day while you're taking your morning shower or driving into work. That's not planning; it's functioning. Coaches and wrestlers who do no more planning than that have lots of ups and downs. Their actions are based on day-to-day feelings rather than well-thought-out goals and the tasks they need to do to achieve those goals. You have to see the bigger picture and not be knocked off course by temporary moods or problems. Planning means taking systematic steps to get where you want to go. I know I want my wrestling program to be on top at the end of the season, so that's what I plan for—success. The graphs in figures 5.1 and 5.2 indicate an athlete's levels of readiness for competitions. In the rest of this chapter, I'll explain what planning I do each year.

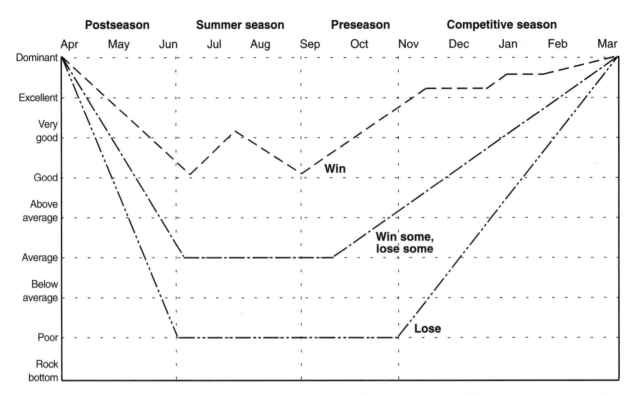

During April and May if competing in freestyle and Greco-Roman matches, drops in the curve would be less. Basically the graph is a replica of the letter W with a few peaks and valleys. Bottom teams have peaks and valleys that are too steep.

Figure 5.1   Levels of readiness for competition for wrestlers only

LOGISTICS

Part of the plan for success involves having sufficient foresight to avoid recurring problems. These minor issues may not seem like all that much, but when you add them up over the course of the season, you realize the big toll they took on your program. A cracked water pipe in the locker room, a shortage of headgear and no money to purchase any more, a misinterpretation of a rule that leads to a match forfeiture, and a mix-up in hotel accommodations are all perils of poor planning. You may not enjoy handling the nuts and bolts of managing a wrestling program, but someone on your staff had better do it. The better it's done, the more trouble-free you'll be.

You should plan to address these general logistics:

✓ Facility maintenance

✓ Equipment maintenance

✓ Medical screenings and insurance

✓ Rules

✓ Budgets

✓ Schedules

✓ Travel

Facilities and Equipment

Your practice facility and equipment must be available and in good condition before the first day of practice. These are the minimal necessities to have ready:

- **Wrestling mats.** These must be ready for another season's use and abuse. Examine them at least two months before the first practice. If you have doubts about whether the mats will hold up, have them replaced or refinish them before you get started.

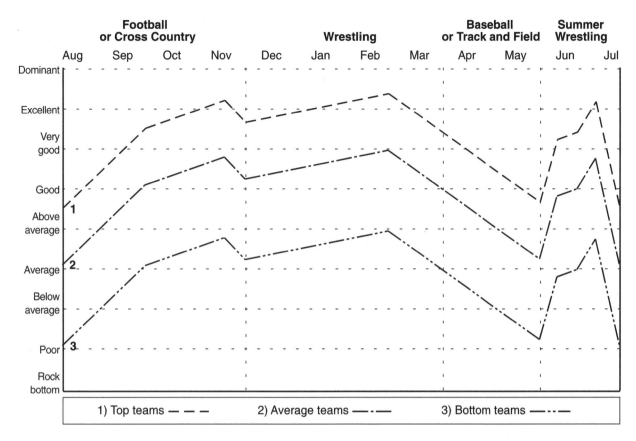

The reason dominance isn't reached here is because of the level of the expectations of athletics at this stage.
One thing to take into account is that even though the graph lines are similar in peaks and valleys, the top teams/individuals will be going two to three weeks longer. Therefore, adjustments should be made for better performances when they really count.

Figure 5.2   Levels of readiness for competition for a three-sport athlete

- **Mat cleaner/disinfectant.** All it takes is one slip up, and your whole team could be wiped out. Keep the mats clean by having plenty of disinfectant on hand and using it between each practice session and at other appropriate times.

- **Laundry system.** Wrestlers' practice wear, match uniforms, and towels should all be properly laundered every day. If they aren't, rashes and infections will develop and spread. Good hygiene can't be compromised.

- **Headgear and mouthguards.** When equipment can prevent unnecessary injuries, why not use it? This equipment is especially important in preventing the transmission of blood-borne diseases.

- **Match uniforms.** If you need new ones, order them well ahead of the start of the season. Check that sizes are correct. If you need to special order, do so in plenty of time.

- **Wrestling shoes.** Function, not fashion, should be the primary concern here. Remember that proper fit is required for proper function.

- **Practice gear.** I recommend wrestlers wear a short-sleeve T-shirt (single thickness), athletic shorts, briefs (first choice) or athletic supporter (second choice), and white athletic socks.

- **Knee pads.** Have plenty of sleeve-type pads available to help protect the wrestler's Achilles heel.

- **Used crash pads** (for example, gymnastics pits).

- **Stationary bike.** You don't need the most expensive or high-tech bike, but you

Stationary bikes often work well for warm-ups, extra conditioning, or workouts for an injured athlete. Here former NCAA champion Bill Zadick is doing some extra conditioning on the Airdyne.

should have one that's in good working order available for extra conditioning, rehabilitation, and facilitating weight loss.

If you have the funds, set up conditioning stations near the practice area and have these items available:

- Station 1: Ropes for climbing (knee-high to ceiling with safety mats underneath)
- Station 2: Jump ropes
- Station 3: Chin bars
- Station 4: Dip bars
- Station 5: Dumbbells (a few sets for arm pummeling and rowing)
- Station 6: Lifeline workout apparatus (for pummeling and forearm conditioning)

If you have some extra money, Adam takedown machines and throwing dummies are excellent training tools. A cheap but effective alternative is an old football dummy. I trained with one of these on a 12' by 12' mat in my basement throughout my competitive high school, college, and international wrestling years.

Having that 12' by 12' mat at home had a lot to do with my success as a wrestler. I could work out away from school (my dad carried extra insurance after witnessing a few of my early workouts). Because of the dimensions of the mat and the proximity of the surrounding basement walls, I developed the habit of circling towards the center, which saved considerably on home repairs and injuries. The smaller mat is a big help in learning how to put the finishing touches on your opponent. It was a key to my success in immediate finishing. Lastly, Hammer Strength training equipment has been a favorite of Iowa wrestling for the last several years. Jeff Conner at Hammer

Terry Brands uses some after-practice strength and conditioning routines that the great ones use to get great.

Strength has been closely associated with wrestling for many years and can give you insights into this equipment. You can call 800-872-1543 for information.

Medical Screening and Insurance

I'm not qualified to discuss all of the reasons and ways, but having competed in and coached this sport for 38 years, I do know that wrestlers need a complete physical exam before each season. Iowa's recruited athletes undergo an extensive medical screening process as soon as they set foot on campus. Rules allow schools to do medical checks on recruits even when they are on campus for their official and unofficial visits. A medical check is a good idea anytime you have a concern about an athlete's physical status.

One very basic reason for arranging physicals for all wrestlers is that you want to be as sure as possible that all of the athletes can endure the workouts they're about to begin. My early season conditioning and test workouts aren't easy. I build athletes' fitness base through extensive endurance-type activities.

Early Season Workouts

The following workouts become very competitive for the athletes and bring the most effort out of them. The morning and afternoon workouts are usually not done on the same day, but could be if necessary. Be aware that these workouts also may cause athletes to lose some extra weight. The early season screening will tell you each wrestler's percent body fat, so you'll know when weight loss is in danger of becoming muscle and energy loss.

Morning Workout (6:15 a.m.)

1. Light stretching in wrestling room.
2. Athletes go outdoors and jog to intramural field (1/4 mile).
3. Full stretching.
4. Run six laps of 1/3 mile each for total of two miles.

5. Pummel hard with partner for five minutes.
6. Various conditioning drills for five minutes.
7. Four 150-yard sprints.
8. Jog back to wrestling room.
9. Three rope climbs of 25 feet each.

Afternoon Workout (3:30 p.m.)

1. Short warm-up and stretching.
2. Techniques and tactics for 30 minutes.
3. Combat for 30 minutes.

Note. Have a team physician or trainer available or on call at every practice and match. In addition, a coach or trainer skilled in current athletic training procedures should be on-site.

As part of your planning, inform athletes well before they arrive for early season workouts what kind of shape they'll need to be in. All of my returning athletes and most of my recruits show up in good condition because they know what to expect and know what a price they'll pay if they aren't in good condition. Walk-ons, however, often show up inadequately prepared from a fitness standpoint, and those who do often walk-off.

A Lesson in Preparation

We had a recruit once who showed up for the first practice in poor condition, thinking that he could get by on his wrestling skills alone. He soon realized the mistake he'd made, and he quit at the end of our early season conditioning program, saying, "I've just done as much work during this early season training period than I've ever done before in a whole season. I'm through." Although he never wrestled for Iowa, this young man has stayed in touch and speaks with great respect for the work that the wrestlers put in. Furthermore, the lesson that he learned from his experience with us—the need to be prepared before pursuing anything worthwhile—has served him well in his subsequent academic and professional pursuits.

Medical insurance for wrestlers isn't optional. If your school or club doesn't provide it, make wrestlers show evidence of their coverage. A signed statement by their parents confirming their son's coverage is also a good precaution.

Rules

Another aspect of planning is staying informed of and in compliance with the rules. Wrestling isn't like driving a car, where once you learn the rules of the road you have to brush up on your knowledge only when you have to renew your license. You can pretty much expect that the driving rules that applied last year will apply this year and the next; no such luck in wrestling.

School-based wrestling programs have more administrative, off-the-mat rules than they do on-the-mat rules. Wrestling has so many rules that it's hard to keep them all straight, much less comply with them. Conference, state, and national athletic, coaching, and wrestling organizations all have standards in place. It's your duty to keep up on them.

Lack of communication and assumptions based on incomplete or incorrect information can get you in trouble. For instance, several of the schools in the Big Ten conference (including Iowa), faced penalties because a rule interpretation made by the Big Ten was unacceptable to the NCAA. The Big Ten office failed to keep its member school athletic programs aware of the differences in interpretations, so we just assumed that the approach we were taking was acceptable. It wasn't. Assumptions aren't good enough, real facts and interpretations are the only acceptable option.

Take a few days before each competitive season to get all of the current guidelines for your wrestling program. If there's a problem, correct it immediately. Don't wait until someone else brings it to your attention. On-the-mat rules are less susceptible to change, but keep your staff and team updated on all recent wrestling rule changes. Wrestling rules may vary somewhat according to the level of competition and type of event.

Budget

Many wrestling programs have been scaled back or cut in recent years. In certain places wrestling is the poor boy on the block. The programs that are showcased by the athletic department always get the biggest piece of the pie. With gender equity requirements, women's sports are being created and funded while several men's sports are being dropped.

Because of this situation, getting the funding and scholarships necessary to make ends meet can be difficult. Coaches can make all the difference as to whether their programs will survive. Do your homework to counter those who would gain at your wrestlers' expense, and keep your program functioning at a level that makes it very difficult for the administration to diminish or cut it.

If you do have adequate resources for equipment, staff, travel, and so forth, you may have them for only a short time, unless you set up a budget and stay within it. Financial planning expertise isn't needed, just common sense and some restraint. Don't hedge your bets and spend the money you're expecting to raise later. Don't toss out adequate equipment and replace it with the latest models each year. Be responsible with your budget, and, with some good planning, your program should get by okay.

Schedules

Who you compete against and when you compete against them is critical. If you underschedule or overschedule in terms of the level and number of competitions, you'll see the consequences by the end of the season. Performance will drop, injuries will increase, motivation will suffer, and so on. Although some of you may have little control or flexibility over who you compete against, use whatever influence you have to ensure a good schedule.

The schedule that's best for a veteran, championship-caliber team isn't the same as the best schedule for a young, good squad. For example, when all of Iowa's 1991 NCAA Championship team returned for the 1992 season, I scheduled more competition and less practice, and the team made a couple road trips to promote the program, as well as the sport. With an inexperienced team, you want to ease into the season by wrestling against good but not great competition, spending more time on practice, and having as few as distractions as possible.

A good event for Iowa is the National Duals Meet, an in-season multiteam competition involving some of the best teams and individuals in the country. This event not only generates fan interest for the sport in the middle of the season, but also prepares the teams and athletes for the conference and NCAA meets held several weeks later. Away matches and matches against rivals are also important to establish a successful routine on the road and handle the adversity of opposing team's fans.

Sometimes you might schedule an opponent for less obvious reasons. For instance, at the college level, it always helps to wrestle in or near areas of strong recruiting. You want potential recruits and present team members to be able to bring their family and friends and see the team in competition. Wrestlers like to know that they'll get to wrestle near home if they attend your school. At the high school level, you may schedule an opponent from the closest major city to gain visibility for your program. Being seen by some writers from metropolitan papers may help you get some attention in the state rankings.

Another side of the scheduling coin is entertaining the offers by others who want to compete against you. Be selective, keeping in mind the type of team you have and how you want it to develop during the season. Because of limitations on the number of events, you can't accept all of the offers, even when they are attractive to you. The two key guidelines in setting up a schedule are to take few if any long road trips and to underschedule rather than overschedule (get quality, not quantity). The lack of long road trips allows for more practice time at home, and keeping the schedule from being too difficult gives you time to experiment and make necessary adjustments during the season. The team's academic area will suffer less with this philosophy as well.

Promotion and Competition

The 1994 NCAA wrestling championships were held in Chapel Hill, North Carolina. It was the first time that this area of the country had hosted the tournament. Anticipating some difficulty in getting exposure and fans for this event, University of North Carolina coach Bill Lam asked me in '93 whether we would come and wrestle his team early in the '93–'94 season. He felt that the Iowa wrestling program could generate the attention and excitement for wrestling in that part of the country, which would spur sales for the NCAA tournament. Unfortunately, I couldn't find any way for us to add North Carolina to our schedule that season. With only 16 dates allowed and our previous commitments to conference and other opponents, it was impossible to accept Coach Lam's invitation, even though it was a good strategy by the host school for promotional purposes. From the way our team performed at this NCAA site, we could have used the trip to familiarize ourselves with the arena.

Travel Planning Tips

✓ Check with informed people about the condition of the hotels you are considering and make sure that its upkeep, restaurant facilities, and location are adequate.

✓ Stay at hotels that offer recreational facilities such as a pool, whirlpool, and sauna for physical and mental preparation and therapy. *Due to new rules governing last-second weight loss, some of these facilities might be off-limits. Make sure proper instruction takes place with your team to avoid problems.*

✓ Set departure and travel times that get you to the site in time for proper rest and training. Check on access to the arena or gym before the competition.

PERSONNEL

Logistical planning is important, but the most important planning involves the wrestling program's most important resource, the athletes. Immediately after a season you should begin planning who will fill each of the weights on next year's team. Get to know each individual on the upcoming squad. Give your wrestlers guidance regarding what techniques they should work on during the off-season, what camps they might attend, and what conditioning program to follow. Make sure they have a facility where they can work out. Be available at certain times of the week if any wrestlers want to consult you. Ask for a monthly progress report from each athlete during the off-season. This report keeps you in touch with all team members, and it makes them feel more accountable for adhering to their off-season work.

Season Guide for Wrestlers

Most successful businesses have a company operating manual. Each employee is given one of these manuals when hired and is expected to abide by the policies in working toward the goal of improving the corporate culture and performance. Iowa does the same with its team. I've included a couple of guides from our '78-'79 and '96-'97 seasons as examples. Note the change in emphasis 18 years later. The theme for the season should be carefully thought out and explained in simple terms. It should motivate and challenge your team and raise realistic and idealistic expectations.

1978–1979 season—my second year as head coach

Becoming #1 Individually

The following are minimum guidelines for the sport of wrestling at the national championship level. Anything short of this training hurts your chances, anything greater helps your chance in obtaining a national championship.

After coaching and observing the recent World Championships in Mexico, I have concluded that there are certain skills in wrestling that must be mastered for good success in any high-level competitions. For standing wrestling the following are essential: (1) Being able to push or stand up to your opponent with good control ties, being able to use inside controls for pushing, pummelling and control ties (two-on-ones, underlocks, etc.) for control of your opponent. As these control ties are mastered, offensive takedowns must be attempted and completed from them; (2) the standing single-leg and finishes must be mastered; (3) defense from everywhere on the feet is a must—first to keep your opponent from scoring and second to *score* on your opponent from your defenses. Snapdowns, two-on-ones, and front headlocks must be mastered while your opponent is attempting to score on you. *Position* and *balance* are musts while your opponent is attempting to finish single-legs, double-legs, and high-crotches.

Of course, each wrestler is an individual and can use whatever works best for him. However, the above must be mastered as well.

For collegiate wrestling, the escape is another must. I suggest the stand-up with good hand control. Being able to flow from one thing to another is also very important in underneath wrestling, in case you are blocked at a certain time. *One must master getting to his base position when flat on the mat.*

Riding and pinning are two areas that make your wrestling more fun and interesting, but more than that, you can mentally break your opponents easier than any other positions.

Your best learning experiences when wrestling one-on-one are to wrestle in all positions and fight in all positions to be able to be familiar with them. If one quits in practices in any area, his chances of success in matches will be less.

To learn the skills talked about so far, one must drill these positions, both easy and as well tough. Put and start yourself there.

Physical Condition Aspects

When one gets tired, his performance is definitely decreased. Your ability is brought down to a lower level. Don't cheat yourself here!

Superior strength and overall cardiovascular conditioning are musts! Weight training and running greatly aid the wrestler for this type of combat.

Each one of us must analyze ourselves and definitely work on our weaknesses, especially in the pre-season. The three areas for analysis are in our wrestling, our strengths, and our wind and muscle conditioning. Ask the coaches for advice in your weaknesses.

Workouts

Space your workouts for maximum results. Your body needs to recuperate for best gains. The easier the workout, the less time needed to recuperate and vice-versa. I suggest early morning and our 4:00 workout if working twice, hard. Have at least five to six hours for recuperation when working hard. A suggestion is to wrestle one-on-one hard one day and the next drill on technique and wrestle hard in specific positions only.

A good diet and weight control is a must for top wrestling. Discipline is the key here.

Priorities When Training

The use of alcohol and drugs will hinder your chances of becoming a national champ. Know what and when you can do when socializing in terms of not detracting from becoming a national champ. Excessive drugs, alcohol, and late hours detract!

I will not tolerate drugs. If you have a problem, quit; before it is a real problem. Remember you're here for the following:

(1) to get a good education and to graduate

(2) to become a national champ

(3) to enjoy the *goods* of college life.

The following is the schedule for pre-season starting Sept. 18 and ending Oct. 19:

Monday, Sept. 18

Distance work for building of endurance—4 miles

Tuesday, Sept. 19

Light weight day for muscular endurance and strength. Weight lifting using light weights and maximum reps. Jog 1/2 to 1 mile before lifting for warm-up. Time: 1 hour. 5:00–6:00 video tapes (World and Olympic Championships)

1996–1997 season—my final year as head coach

The Dome . . . 97

Most of you probably don't realize the surroundings you are heading into for this year's upcoming NCAAs. The current wrestlers making history on the mats will be viewed by many that have made mat history in the past. Of course, this always somewhat happens, but in Iowa in the 40s, 50s, and 60s, this particular area, along with Cornell College in Mt. Vernon, was distinctively nationally known for its collegiate wrestling. Sure we are familiar with Iowa's and Iowa State's history somewhat, but you'll be wrestling right in an area that wrestling was "King" and many names were immortalized in wrestling history.

We should be ready to impress the "immortals" and yes, all the people in the stands, with what has developed over the years in the science and development of our sport and as you being outstanding individuals and performers.

A couple of examples of past history are the following: In 1950, the last time UNI hosted the NCAAs, they won the tournament with three champions, two runners-up, one third, and one fourth when the number of weight classes was only eight. Cornell College, this same year, was third with one champion, one second, and two fourths. The University of Iowa placed sixth with one champion—Joe Scarpello. Another interesting item here is the fact that Joe Williams's high school coach, Bill Weick, wrestled for UNI (at that time called Iowa State Teachers College) and won two NCAA titles during this era. I could go on and on with famous wrestling names from this era but yes, it is now, and the past is the past.

With you I'm concerned with what is now and what is upcoming and remember, you are going into famous wrestling country . . . so be ready.

Some of you are trying to gain eligibility and others are close to losing it, so at least give yourself the "chance of opportunity." Use the resources available but more important, use your own resources . . . "Make your breaks . . . time marches on . . . I love you guys."

1996–97 IOWA WRESTLING TEAM RULES

Rules

Starting eight seasons ago, rules concerning drugs, alcohol, etc., were put into affect by the University. You have to sign them to be able to participate so I'm assuming you know them. I will go over them often to remind you of the consequences. Generally remember—three strikes and you're out! As in past years, the following hasn't changed (don't forget why you are here):

1) to get a good education and to graduate
2) to become a national champion and Olympic champion
3) to enjoy the goods of college life

Philosophy

Most of you have become entertaining in your wrestling by putting on a spectacular display of great intense wrestling, dominating your opponents. For those of you who haven't yet, it takes a tremendous commitment in attitude and spirit to do so. Don't be left behind . . . join the bandwagon! It can be exciting and rewarding. Don't forget our educational goals of graduating with the highest GPA possible and of course, in areas that will set us great for the future.

We are once again instilling fear in our opponents and remember, we must never be cowardly, only make our opponents that way.

Notes

Common time for wrestling, conditioning, or lifting is 3:30 P.M. to 5:30 P.M., however, this can be done at any other times except on mandatory dates.

Body fat and weight should be reduced during pre-season.

If running at night, wear reflectors.

Major rule changes for 1996-97 will be discussed during pre-season.

1996–97 tentative schedule

Strength, conditioning, and skill work—maximum 8 hrs/wk supervised for the dates of August 26th through September 15th (2 hrs max skill work).

[Here you should include the season's wrestling schedule, including mandatory meetings, practice schedule, and competitive schedule.]

When making the season practice schedule, the best approach is to start at the end of the season and work back to day one. You know where you want to be at the end of the season, so practices need to pave the way for getting there. Make a note with your practice schedule that the season plan is subject to change on any given day as needs arise. I'll get into the specifics of practice planning in chapter 6.

Educational Opportunities

In my experience, the more good and useful information you give athletes, the stronger your program will be. Encourage questions, provide expert speakers and instructional materials, and counsel athletes yourself, when necessary. The subjects might include nutrition, weight control, wrestling technique and tactics, training, social responsibility, academic requirements, and a whole assortment of other topics. A wrestler who isn't motivated to increase his knowledge in these areas probably also lacks the desire and discipline to succeed on the wrestling mat. The point of providing this information is not to make every athlete a genius, but rather to give each wrestler a chance to get the most out of his abilities.

Support Staff

The second most important personnel in your program are the other members of your staff. Assistant coaches, trainers, academic counselors, and managers must all be informed and work toward the same goals. This group of people needs to pull in the same direction or smooth operation and good results will be difficult to achieve. Differences of opinion are okay and can be healthy, but good communication and a willingness to support the consensus is a must.

SUMMARY

The old saying that "a failure to plan is planning to fail" is as true in wrestling as it is in anything else. Doing paperwork and checking equipment aren't what most coaches prefer to do, but it sure beats the alternative. The time you devote to logistical and personnel planning will save you tenfold the time you'll spend and the headaches you'll get trying to manage each area when problems arise.

I covered the main areas of season planning in this chapter:

- Equipment and facilities
- Medical screening and insurance
- Rules
- Budget

- Schedules
- Wrestler education
- Support staff

It's impossible to cover everything you need to plan for in one chapter, but if you plan effectively in each of these areas, you'll be off to a great start for the wrestling season.

Chapter

6

PLANNING FOR PRACTICES

When the season plan is in place, you begin focusing on individual practice sessions. The practices you develop should be consistent with your objectives and time of the season. For example, during midseason, my team has winter break and few or no matches, so practices become the wrestlers' number one priority. The team goes back to work on fundamentals, and I adjust the training to correct problems I've seen in the first four to six weeks of competition.

In high school, you have a shorter break, but I recommend doing much the same thing. Schedule lesser or no opponents during this time so you can adjust your training and practice schedule. Maybe you need to make line-up changes, allow injured athletes to rest and rehabilitate, or develop a more positive attitude. With careful planning and wise use of this valuable time period, you can get the edge needed to achieve great things in the second half of the season and during postseason, when it really counts.

EARLY SEASON PRACTICES

The first two or three days of practice should be learning experiences, more so for coaches than for athletes. Most coaches don't realize this fact and take control right away, trying to teach their wrestlers too many things in too little time. What coaches should do during the first few practice sessions is supervise and observe, not try to teach.

Through close observation and proper evaluation of wrestlers at this time, you can make better decisions for individuals and the entire team. I recommend spending this time filling each weight class and dividing up your team into smaller groups according to individual needs. For example, certain wrestlers may be great in the standing position, but need some help with their technique in the bottom position. Your initial observation will also help you determine which wrestlers have little or no experience so that you can help them stay injury-free and put them with other wrestlers against whom they can have some success.

If available, assistant coaches can be assigned to each of the groups to provide maximum individual instruction. I use a curtain to partition the groups from one another and for some privacy whenever the team has to share the facility with another group. You also can use a curtain to isolate individuals or activities that could be distracting to others.

The initial analysis of the team should include evaluation of these seven essential ingredients of good wrestling:

- Standing wrestling
- Underneath wrestling as well as coming out and keeping the opponent's legs out
- Strength
- General conditioning
- Flexibility
- Nutrition
- Attitude

I make a chart and rate each wrestler on these attributes and then combine the information for a composite look at the team. Remember, these are minimum characteristics for wrestling, a starting point. If your team has some deficiencies, it's best to learn about them at the outset, so you can correct them as quickly as possible.

Standing Wrestling

In standing wrestling, leg attacks are by far the most common and most successful for win-

ning wrestling. Two of Iowa's all-time greats, Jim Zalesky and Rico Chiapparelli, came into the program with heart and the desire to be great. They both had great scoring tactics; however, many of their skills were from the defensive positions. Although they had some early success, it wasn't enough to set them apart from many of the nation's best. They both worked extremely hard and developed offensive leg attacks that were dependable in tough situations, which consequently put them with the elite of wrestling.

Four-time All-American, three-time NCAA champion, and NCAA outstanding wrestler Jim Zalesky executes one of his leg attacks—something he needed to help his overall success at the college level.

Rico Chiapparelli, NCAA champion, best known for his exotics, developed leg attacks so he could have extra success at the upper levels of his wrestling competitions.

Along with the offensive leg attacks comes the defense tactic of keeping people off your legs. A wrestler does so by having good hand control, head and shoulder positioning, and blocking skills. A wrestler with a good stance and good motion can perform these skills. By doing so correctly, a wrestler will score, usually with go-behinds or snapdowns. These tactics allow for a constant ability to score whether it be offensive and/or defensive.

Underneath Wrestling

The second category, the underneath position, needs to be mastered also. Oftentimes, a dominant wrestler could have this area as his weakness simply because he might not often end up in this position. As coaches, we need to save some part of every practice for this area. I sometimes find this area is a problem for my team because I coach to dominate and usually that means the offensive takedown area and top position.

The best technique to master in the bottom position is the stand-up done with correct hand control. Keeping one's opponent's legs out of yours is the best skill to use while standing up. Sit-outs, switches, and rolls are also easy techniques to learn to be able to help the down position. A combination of all of these tremendously aids your escaping ability. The sit-out with good hand control is probably the easiest escape to learn. Wrestlers must also know how to remove opponents' legs from theirs and/or escape from opponents' legs when the opponents have a firm grasp. Not giving your opponent anything to work with is the best solution most of the time.

In regards to learning how to escape, a great example in Iowa wrestling was Bruce Kinseth. Bruce was one of Iowa's hardest workers. His workouts were legendary, and his intensity and conditioning were phenomenal. The one problem was his underneath position, and the rules at this time put you in the bottom position for either the second or third period. Against the really good wrestlers he sometimes would get ridden for the whole period, therefore, neutralizing his intensity and conditioning.

Bruce Kinseth, former NCAA champion and the NCAA outstanding wrestler in 1979, needed to perfect the escape before his wrestling credentials started adding up.

Coach J. Robinson perfected a sit-out for Bruce, so no one could ride him. All his hard work was finally able to pay off for him; his winning percentage jumped greatly with the development of a single skill. Once his escape was perfected, he finished first in the nation, winning the Most Falls trophy and the Most Outstanding Wrestler award his senior year. He pinned everyone in the Big Ten and NCAA Championships his senior year.

A combination hip-heist movement from underneath is the skill that needs to be perfected in escaping. This skill also is extremely helpful from a defensive position on takedowns as well. When used after the initial counter, it becomes an offensive scoring maneuver. Like a good takedown, the best escape/reversal to use is the one that works.

Strength

Strength is another area that is vital for success. If a wrestler is lucky enough to have the genes that promote muscle and strength development, then this area doesn't require quite as much emphasis. Depending on the wrestler's muscle type, you can point his strength training to where it is most needed— power or endurance. The other benefits of strength training are how it can build up a wrestler's mind and help prevent injuries.

The old Soviet system of athletics emphasized strong body/strong mind preparation at an early age and selected athletes who were

Coach J. Robinson, now at the University of Minnesota, taught some great skills and philosophy to bring an athlete's level of success up.

"naturals" for their sport. Consequently, their training consisted of more sport-specific activities and less general conditioning and training. A good strength training program is typically part of a wrestler's training schedule for power and explosion, which are needed to complete and execute a variety of skills in this sport.

An economical way of gaining strength is to work hard at a specific job that requires heavy lifting, building, or digging. The most strength I ever gained was in the summer between my junior and senior years in high school. The job was working with Martinson Construction Company out of Cedar Falls, Iowa, where I worked with concrete and did a lot of hauling and digging. Instead of strength training that summer, I worked extremely hard at the job and gained tremendous strength (and made money at the same time). Other summers, I worked hard at Wheeler-Braun lumberyard in Waterloo and consequently came off the job more prepared for my wrestling matches. Of course continuing to wrestle during this time (two to three times per week) kept the sport close as well.

Wrestlers should do strength training the whole year to make sure they stay fit and to prevent injuries. Former Iowa two-time NCAA champion Chuck Yagla is a great example of what maintaining your strength can do, especially during the season. Chuck, in his first two years at Iowa, lifted weights in the off-season but didn't continue with this strength training during the competitive season. Chuck also lost quite a bit of weight through the season and his power dropped off as the season was winding down. He did well his freshman and sophomore years, but in his junior year he started a strength program before the season and maintained it through the competitive season. As a result, his performances were much stronger all the way to the end. Chuck won the NCAA Championships in both his junior and senior seasons and was voted outstanding wrestler his final year.

General Conditioning

Conditioning is another one of the essentials. Even though high school matches are only six minutes long, conditioning plays a major role in matches if they are wrestled with intensity. Based on a study I've done, when one athlete is forcing the action to his opponent, conditioning becomes a factor shortly after the four-minute mark. This observation assumes the opponent has been training and has been

Maintaining a strength program throughout the entire season helped Chuck Yagla (two-time NCAA champion) in his junior and senior seasons.

Ten Miles to a Title

Former Iowa NCAA champion Brad Smith, on his initial questionnaire at wrestling practice, stated that he was a self-driver who didn't need the coaches' extra push in the area of conditioning. Left alone, Brad seemed to do less well than he should have. The third period of matches was especially tough for him. During Brad's senior year, former coach Gary Kurdelmeier and myself decided to give him some help to build the edge needed to win. To Brad's credit, he knew he needed to take his training up a notch to be a champion.

Once a week, Brad was dropped off 10 miles outside of town and ran back. This distance was the farthest he had run and required him to move beyond his previous comfort zone of conditioning. By stepping up his conditioning, he also surpassed his previous level of wrestling. In the NCAA finals his senior year, Brad majored his opponent and afterwards credited those 10-mile runs for the improvement in his performance, whether physical or mental.

Brad Smith (left), NCAA champion in 1976, needed that extra coaching to develop his physical and mental ability and get to the top.

put through highly productive wrestling practices. Opponents of less quality are affected sooner. This observation also assumes that the wrestler who is forcing the action has worked to the point that conditioning is not a factor in his situation.

With this fact in mind, an overall goal of my teams is to have my athletes in such good condition that they can perform at their highest level throughout their matches. Initially, not all wrestlers will be willing to work this hard, but even those who don't will benefit from this philosophy. As they witness someone who is training at a high level and see his results, they too are more likely to strive for this goal.

The point you must drive home to your wrestlers is that it's easier to go higher when you start higher; their productivity year-round will be greater if they stay at a higher fitness level year-round. Daily work adds up to a whole lot after a while. Five minutes a day doesn't seem like much, but it equals close to 31 hours of extra work when added up for a whole year. Add that up over an athlete's career in high school, and that's 124 hours of extra work. Add four years of college, and that's 248 extra hours of work.

A wrestler can develop from average to good or good to great with just a bit more time and effort each day. The key here is to teach the athlete how to push himself. Conditioning is usually the difference when it comes down to the fourth, fifth, sixth, or extra minutes in a wrestling match. Building the desire in the athlete to do extra training is a key factor in his achieving a high performance level and should be of highest priority to every wrestling coach. Another key is to actually put more intensity and work in during the same time period on a daily basis.

Flexibility

Flexibility is another trait that needs to be worked on. Most people appreciate the need for power in wrestlers, but flexibility is often overlooked. Many very successful wrestlers over the years could contribute part of their

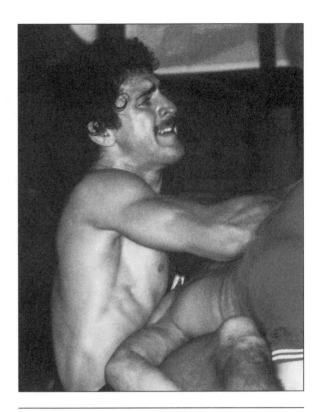

Nick Gallo, former Hofstra NCAA champion and NCAA outstanding wrestler, used his great flexibility to help slick his opponents.

success to their excellent flexibility, even if it hasn't been very apparent. Nick Gallo, former NCAA champion and picked outstanding wrestler at the tournament in the late '70s, used his flexibility and smoothness to great benefit.

Two-time Olympic champion John Smith was able to revolutionize some attack techniques with the help of his body's exceptional flexibility. More recently, two of Iowa's greats have definitely used flexibility to help them win NCAA titles—Lincoln McIlravy and Jeff McGinness.

Using one's flexibility to get into certain positions normally not attacked makes a wrestler feel very powerful. From the bottom position defensively in freestyle, good flexibility can be of great advantage. Being flexible and powerful is a bonus to any wrestler. Besides attacking through offensive maneuvers, flexible wrestlers can be much more effective in counter wrestling and make it very difficult for an opponent to score.

STRETCHING

As one gets older, most everyone will finally realize the importance of muscle and joint flexibility. This is one area that is often overlooked in life and especially in sports. Interestingly, flexibility rates right alongside the necessary ingredients needed for being successful in wrestling. Often, the hardest wrestlers to score on are the ones with great flexibility. Finishing a takedown or turning an opponent can be extremely difficult with a highly skilled and flexible opponent. Stretching is an integral part of warming up and cooling down after practice. It is also something that can be continually used after competitive athletics simply for health reasons.

The following stretches are good ones for use with the sport of wrestling. They are best performed after spending several minutes doing an aerobic-type warm-up. Those can include, but are not limited to, running, biking, rope skipping, and calisthenics.

Letting the body completely hang loose and letting gravity take over will help lengthen and loosen tight areas. A strong chinning bar or other devices that are sufficiently stable will aid this exercise. Light twisting of the trunk and torso is good here, as well as doing knee-to-chest raises while hanging. Circular rotation of most body joints will aid in the warm-up process for wrestlers. Remember to circle both ways. Self/ partner massage is another technique that is helpful.

Other specific stretches that are good for wrestling follow. The final three partner stretches are good for after practice.

Standing hamstring stretch

Exhale when you bend forward. Exhale and bend your knees or round your torso when returning to the upright position.

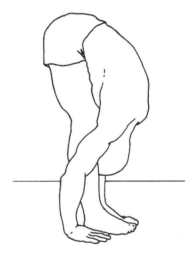

Seated side stretch

Exhale as you extend your upper torso and grasp your foot. Concentrate on keeping your lower back and legs extended and your heels on the floor.

Spinal twist

Exhale as you turn your trunk and gently push on your knee with your elbow.

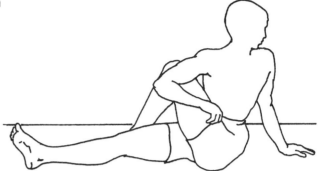

Head bridge

Inhale as you raise your trunk and rest your forehead on the floor.

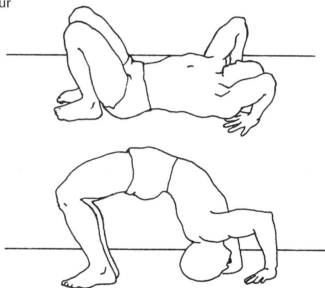

Elbow-head bridge

Inhale, raise your trunk, and rest your forehead on the floor. Then raise one arm at a time and place your forearms on the floor.

Dog stretch

Exhale as you extend your shoulders and press on the floor with your arms to stretch your back.

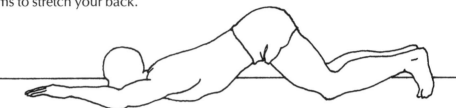

Modified plough

Exhale as you put your hands behind your knees and pull your thighs to your chest.

Reclining hero

Exhale as you continue to lean backward until you are flat on your back. Do not arch your back. Instead, contract your gluteals and rotate your pelvis backward. Do not allow your feet to flare out to the side or your knees to rise off the floor or spread apart.

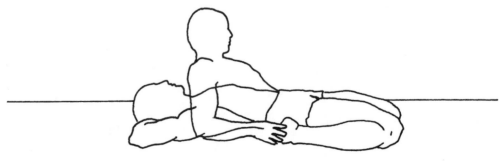

Sitting hamstring stretch with partner

Exhale and keep your legs straight, extend your upper torso, and bend forward at the hips as your partner pushes your upper torso onto your thighs.

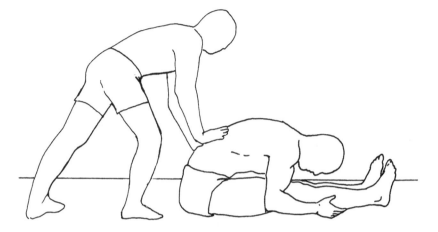

Lying butterfly with partner

Exhale as your partner pushes your legs to the floor. Be sure to communicate with your partner.

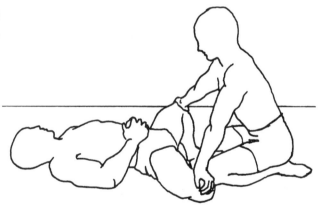

Boston crab partner stretch

Contract your gluteals as your partner anchors your abdomen to the floor with one hand and gently lifts your leg higher with the other. This exercise creates an intense stretch, so be sure to communicate with your partner.

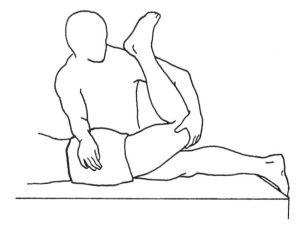

John Smith (bottom), two-time Oklahoma State NCAA champion and two-time Olympic champion, used his incredible flexibility to put himself into scoring positions that started a whole new phase of scoring tactics.

After stretching, do some jogging and complete your workout with a sauna and/or massage and hot shower. For best recuperative results and therapy, finish with a warm or cool shower and ice anything that is hurting or something you want to keep working to the maximum.

Nutrition

Nutrition and weight control are probably the most controversial subjects in wrestling. Of course, the key issue here is weight loss. The image of a dehydrated wrestler wearing a sweatsuit in a hot gym in order to lose weight is not a healthy one for the sport. What wrestling needs to promote in terms of nutrition and weight is fitness and health.

Rules on Weight Control

Following the lead of the National Collegiate Athletic Association, the National Federation of State High School Associations has tightened regulations on weight control in wrestling. The NCAA made eight rule revisions after the deaths of three college wrestlers during weight-loss workouts.

All state associations are now required to develop and use a weight-loss program that discourages severe weight reduction. Each wrestler is also required to establish a certified minimum weight before January 15. Certification at a lower weight is then prohibited during the season. Another rule requires wrestlers to have at least half of their weigh-ins during the season at the minimum weight to be used during the state tournament.

Education is the key here. Athletes and coaches need to understand the importance of proper nutrition and end the training practices that brought about the association of starvation with wrestling. School systems should require nutrition courses. In addition, coaches, especially wrestling coaches, should have classroom-type discussions with their

Wrestling With Weight

If you are a wrestler, you are probably not overweight. But you may have to cut weight to achieve a lower weight standard or else be denied permission to compete. Use the following tips to lose weight healthfully.

• First of all, get a realistic picture of how much weight you need to lose by getting your body fat measured. The absolute minimal weight includes 5 percent fat for men and 12 percent fat for women. The minimum weight recommended for wrestlers commonly includes about 7 percent body fat. Trying to achieve a weight that will result in your having to starve yourself to lose muscle or dehydrate yourself to lose water weight is difficult and can hurt rather than enhance your performance.

If you don't have access to calipers or another means to measure your percent body fat, give yourself the less professional "pinch test." If you can pinch more than half an inch of thickness over your shoulder blade or hips, you can safely lose a little more weight.

• Start to lose weight early in the season or, better yet, before the start of the season. That way you'll have the time to lose weight slowly (one to two pounds per week) and more enjoyably. Your goal is to achieve and stay at your lowest healthy body fat level.

• Remember that it is counterproductive to lose weight rapidly before an event. If you do, depleted muscle glycogen and dehydration will take their tolls. In a study of wrestlers who quickly lost about eight pounds (4.5 percent of their body weight), the wrestlers performed 3.5 percent worse on a six-minute arm crank test designed to be similar to a wrestling competition. These results suggest that rapid weight loss in athletes prior to competition may serve as a detriment rather than offer a competitive advantage.

Athletes who struggle and starve to get to a low weight tend to fool only themselves. Remember, the odds are against the starved wrestler who crash diets to make weight as compared to the well-fueled wrestler who routinely maintains or stays within a few pounds of his wrestling weight during training.

• To lose weight, divide your calorie budget into three parts of the day.

• No matter how much weight you have to lose, be sure to eat at least 1,500 calories of a variety of wholesome foods every day to prevent vitamin, mineral, and protein deficiencies. Do not eliminate any food group.

• Water is not extra weight. Your body stores the precious water in a delicate balance. If you disrupt this balance, you will decrease your ability to exercise at your best. Using diuretics, rubber suits, saunas, whirlpools, or steamrooms to dehydrate yourself is dangerous.

• When replacing sweat loss after workouts, note that juices, sports drinks, and soft drinks all have calories. Ration them wisely! The lowest-calorie fluid replacer is water.

• If you are worried that strict dieting as a teenager will stunt your growth, note that you will catch up after the competitive season. Many wrestlers are short in stature not because of malnutrition but rather because of genetics. They tend to have short parents. Small people often select a low-weight sport because they are more suited for that than for football or basketball.

Adapted, by permission, from N. Clark, 1997, *Nancy Clark's Sports Nutrition Guidebook*, 2d ed. (Champaign, IL: Human Kinetics), 267-268.

Jeff McGinness, two-time Iowa NCAA champion, used his extreme balance and flexibility to score points at crucial times.

athletes about healthy eating and adequate fluid intake.

One key to success is being able to get quality work and effort out of your team on a consistent basis. Without proper nutrition, wrestlers' attentiveness and stamina will fall off drastically, especially late in practice. I constantly read my athletes to gauge when to do a certain workout or conditioning drill and for how long. The more I can keep them working with quality efforts and attentiveness the better they are going to get.

Water availability along with an electrolyte (sports) drink is a must. The drinks should be cold for incentive to drink as well as for recuperation purposes. Disposable cups should be used and not shared. If your water source is a drinking fountain, make sure the water is cold and easily drinkable. Oftentimes in older facilities drinking fountains are nearby but barely working. Keep them usable and clean. Drinking fountains are not for spitting, blowing one's nose, or getting rid of gum or chewing tobacco (which should not be permitted, anyway). Keep tissue and plenty of garbage cans for trash handy.

Coaches should have their athletes' body compositions tested and have all the needed data and calculations for each athlete (more

on pre-match nutrition in chapter 11). The maximum weight loss under normal conditions should be no more than two pounds per week. Within this range, wrestlers should be able to maintain their strength and keep a positive attitude. Don't let the athletes just tell you what they weigh; weight checks are necessary. Keep your eyes open for signs of incorrect weight loss measures or weight loss that is too rapid. Clear warning signs are lack of sweat, jumpy attitude, poorer performance, noticeable changes of body size, and frequent trips to the bathroom.

Because of recent tragedies in the sport involving wrestlers and weight loss, extra emphasis is being placed on education and safety rules. Specific concerns about the role of supplements and possible prescription drugs while training intensely are being looked at as well.

At the University of Iowa we test the body fat composition of our wrestling team once a year, and then periodically check some wrestlers throughout the remainder of the year. Each year in early to mid-September the team has mandatory testing with the team athletic trainer. This is within a month after they have returned to school and right around the start of organized practices. The results are used as a guide for the coaches and medical staff to evaluate the roster and begin making decisions about who will wrestle in which weight class. It also allows enough time to counsel and guide the wrestlers on how to safely and properly lose any extra weight over the next eight to ten weeks leading up to their first competition, which is usually in late November. New weight procedures could make for a possible date change of early testing.

The testing method we use at Iowa is caliper measurement. We have access to underwater weighing equipment, which is supposedly the most accurate measurement of body fat, but we use the calipers for several reasons. First, it is less time consuming for both the athletic trainer and the athlete. Second, calipers are more readily available and the test is easier to perform. Finally, underwater weighing has a high learning curve for those being assessed. If the testee is not well trained in having this done, the results may vary dramatically.

We test six different sites on the body with the calipers and use a formula developed by exercise physiologists which is specific to male high school wrestlers. Although these are collegiate wrestlers we are testing, the difference is believed to be minimal. The six sites we measure are the scapula, triceps, chest, suprailiac (hip), abdomen, and thigh. (See the worksheet that follows.) We also

---

Name: _____   Date: _____

Determination of the Fat Content for Collegiate Wrestlers by Use of Skinfold Calipers

Scapular fold	_____ . _____ (mm) × .0746 =	_____ . _____	
Triceps fold	_____ . _____ (mm) × .0769 =	_____ + _____	
Chest fold	_____ . _____ (mm) × .1483 =	_____ + _____	
Suprailiac fold	_____ . _____ (mm) × .1602 =	_____ + _____	
Abdominal fold	_____ . _____ (mm) × .1524 =	_____ + _____	
Thigh fold	_____ . _____ (mm) × .1020 =	_____ + _____	

Total from above   =   _____ . _____

Add   +   3 . 157

** Percent fat **   =   _____ . _____

Estimated Percent Fat From Total Skinfold   _____ . _____

Body weight _____ pounds (BW)

Lean body weight (LBM)   =   BW   −   (% fat   ×   BW   )

_____   =   _____   −   _____   ×   _____

Ideal weight at 5% fat   =   LBM   /   .95

_____   =   _____   /   .95

Determination of fat percentage is a fluctuating assessment and as such can only be viewed accurately as it relates to many such determinations. Ideal weight is based on the assumption that LBM (which is the weight of the body made up of muscle, bone, fluids, etc.) is the weight component that will keep constant and that only your fat weight will be reduced to a minimal value. That assumption is not valid for the real world and that is why many determinations need to be made.

measure their body weight and use the body fat percentage to estimate the "ideal" weight of the wrestler. The ideal weight is theoretically what the wrestler would weigh if they dropped their fat percentage down to five percent fat, which is the figure recommended for college-age athletes not to drop below. For high school athletes, it is recommended that they not drop below seven percent body fat.

In an attempt to be consistent among team members and from one reading to the next on the same athlete, we have an experienced technician perform the tests on all the athletes each time. In our case, the team athletic trainer performs all of the testing.

We recommend that the athletes be tested in the morning hours before they have eaten or worked out. It is important that they are well hydrated since a dehydrated state can skew skinfold readings. This is also when a most accurate weight can be assessed. It is possible and highly likely that with new procedures for making weight, hydration testing will be used along with skinfold measurement.

Attitude

Proper attitude is the last but certainly not the least ingredient for wrestling success. This trait affects all other areas. Without the proper attitude, a wrestler will only go so far. Physical ability can make a wrestler a winner early on in his career, but at more advanced levels where the difference in talent narrows, talent alone won't do it. Your athletes have to be motivated to a very high level for them to be champion wrestlers. Their competitive abilities must be brought out of them through an internal desire to excel and maximize their abilities.

Through observation and good communication you can tell which athletes need to work on their attitude. Through team and individual discussions, you can bring about big improvements. Even highly motivated wrestlers need personal attention, so don't overlook anyone on the team. You can address attitude in many ways, but it starts at the top, so make sure you (the coach) represent what you want your wrestlers to accomplish.

PRACTICES

Productive practices are essential to your overall success. Administrators' current emphasis on paperwork oftentimes loads down a coach so much outside of the practice room that it's hard to get out from behind a desk. Put nonessential paperwork on hold, and see to it that your athletes have sufficient practice time. Wrestling has no shortcuts, especially when it comes to practicing. Be sure to make time for good hard work on the mats; it can't take second place to administrative work.

Your program should be such that your athletes know what they should be doing year-round. When coaches aren't available, wrestlers should understand and do the work needed to prepare themselves for future competitions. During the season, coaches take a more active role in organizing, structuring, motivating, and teaching team members to maximize their development in the time allotted. When the regular season starts, practices should be organized so that athletes have a general feel for and understanding of the structure.

A typical practice follows this timeline:

3:30 Athletes gather on bleachers in wrestling room. The coach discusses details of the upcoming week such as practice schedule, weight classes, team travel, and academics. This business meeting sometimes becomes a lecture for whatever is needed. This part of the practice normally lasts 10 to 15 minutes maximum, except for lecture days and when extra time is needed to get certain points across. I may have the wrestlers demonstrate skills or mistakes to make the whole group aware of a general concern.

3:45 The wrestlers run a few laps around the practice room just to get their heart rates moving and their bodies stretching. Then the team meets in a semicircle to go over any skills or areas that need special attention. Athletes then do drills to work on those areas.

4:15 Athletes are now warmed up after the learning and drill sessions. At this point, athletes perform additional warm-ups and drills at a moderate to live wrestling intensity.

4:30 The athletes take a water break.

4:40 The athletes engage in combative wrestling; this wrestling is sometimes structured, sometimes on their own, sometimes a combination of the two. There are no major coaches' breaks during this time. Once the hard work begins, it keeps going! The only breaks are for recuperation and water.

5:30 The athletes now do their conditioning and strength training exercises, often including hard running, rope climbing, wrestling stance movement, execution, and hand fighting drills.

5:45 Practice ends with reminders and other important words from coaches. Instill an attitude that even though practice is over little extras can be personally done, followed by a cool-down process of jogging and stretching. This cool-down step involves many things that are important for body and mind recuperation and rehabilitation to prepare for tomorrow's training. This is a real key for success to being able to get after it day after day if needed and wanted. Ice, heat, massage, hygiene, nutrition, team morale, and rest are the keys to coming back ready the next day.

Each practice must accomplish important team and individual objectives. The whole team must have spent some quality time in the standing position as well in the underneath position in every practice. Also, if I notice that one young man got beat up and wasn't able to execute any holds in the practice, he and I will stay afterwards to perform some execution drills so he gets experience and accomplishes something from the practice. For learning purposes, never let a practice go by where an athlete fails to have the experience of executing holds.

Practices should be similar so the structure is understandable. Don't make practices

Lincoln McIlravy, three-time Iowa NCAA champion and two-time USA freestyle champion, uses his flexibility to flurry in and out of scoring positions.

too predictable, however. Keep the athletes guessing a little so they don't get too comfortable. I rarely let them know what's next. If they know exactly what to expect, they hold back until the end. For example, if they are going to run 10 sprints, the majority of athletes will hold back until sprints 8, 9, or 10. On the other hand, if they think that they're going to run one sprint all-out, they run the first as hard as the tenth. This way you get maximum effort in all 10 sprints, not just the last two or three.

During practices, assess what is being accomplished. Practice is for learning attacks and scoring. Don't waste practice time with poor execution. The athletes must always be going for scoring maneuvers and creating action and counter action. If you observe a lack of intensity or very little being accomplished, step in and let the team know you want to see better focus and more excitement in the room. Sometimes we are our own worst enemies by not making sure our athletes are making accomplishments and having the proper attitude during their workouts.

Early Season Practices

When you observe your team's traits through close observation during the first few days of practice, keep your thoughts to yourself at this point so that the athletes' performance and effort aren't influenced by your initial impressions. Once you've made a solid evaluation and gained the knowledge needed about your team, set a good base for all of your athletes. Work on endurance conditioning and stamina during early season practices. Weight control can be positively affected by these types of workouts, if supported by good nutrition.

Basic drills and holds should be emphasized now as well. Even when an athlete's level of conditioning is low, he can perform many of the skill and drill activities if the practices are structured properly. A low level of conditioning may require a lower level of intensity and fewer repetitions or shorter time periods for drills, however. Remember to use the same structure noted earlier to keep practices flowing properly (business → warm-up → drilling → final warm-ups → combat → conditioning → cool-down).

Periodic weight checks help put and keep your athletes on schedule. At the same time, a strength maintenance program should be started to prevent any declines in strength. The first part of practices should emphasize the skills needed for that season's team. Some skills are always emphasized, such as leg tackles and hand control, but others may be stressed depending on the group of wrestlers. When daily, early season practices are over, the athletes should have burned a large number of calories, lost some weight if needed, gained considerable stamina, and learned or improved their wrestling skills.

Tryouts should be held immediately following the early season, or just before it ends. Every coach has a preference about how to conduct tryouts. An extensive number of matches is not necessary. The important thing is that wrestlers who are battling to make the team get enough opportunities to prove they

Quick Reference Chart

Business	15 minutes
Techniques and tactics	20 minutes
Drilling	20 minutes
Combat	45 minutes
Conditioning and strength	15 minutes
Note: Thorough warm-ups and cool-downs must be included. These times are just average numbers.	

deserve a roster spot, either through competitions or tryouts. Sometimes it can get rather difficult in this area of your program, so I usually leave it to the consistency of the attitudes of the athletes on which direction to go.

Midseason Practices

After a few early season competitions and several weeks of practice, a coach should do a more thorough analysis of what the team needs to have a good year. At this point, the team is starting to take shape. Pay special attention to back-up wrestlers to keep their interest and motivation at a high level, and try to finalize any lineup changes.

Identify any major team vulnerabilities or recurring errors and do everything possible to correct them. Start pointing out individual needs as well. A little less talk and more corrective action should be taking place at this time of year. Conditioning and intensity are stepped up, and practices are longer, which results in a greater workload. This is the point when a wrestler who needs to gain ground can make it up through the additional daily practice minutes. Iowa's midseason corresponds with winter break. Because school is not in session, the team has two practices a day and some of the best workouts of the year.

Late Season Practices

The last two months of the season involve hard work, peaking training, and making the final changes before tournament time. At this point, you hope that no changes are needed because they can create some dissension on a team, and it's crucial that everyone on the team is pulling in the same direction going into the post-season tournaments. Any weight or nutrition problems should be eliminated by now. Discipline and keeping up with schoolwork need to be emphasized. To keep the team focused, the coaches start sharing motivating stories involving wrestlers who have performed well late in the season and then carried that on to win in the Big Ten and NCAA meets.

No more stamina drills are needed at this point except in special cases. The wrestling done in these practices should be motivating and injury free. This type of wrestling builds the confidence needed for individual success. Strength training is done a couple of times per week: a heavy lifting session five or six days before competition and a circuit training session two or three days before competition. Keeping up strength is very important, both from a physical and mental standpoint. Sprints at the end of practice are good now. The focus of workouts should be on reaching an explosive power level instead of stamina building.

Emphasize rest, sleep, diet, and nutrition. You want your wrestlers feeling extremely healthy, with few aches and pains. If a minor injury happens now, it's easier for athletes to shrug it off if they've peaked right. *A coach should concentrate on his athletes feeling great, even if that means backing off on an individual and team basis.*

Practices are now much shorter in length; Iowa wrestlers have two-a-day practices, but never for two days in a row. You don't want the athletes tired, so if mornings are the time for the extra workouts, alternating days will keep the athletes feeling fresher. On two-a-day practice days, the morning workouts can be accomplished in 45 to 60 minutes, and the afternoon workouts should take 75 to 90 minutes maximum. (These time periods include a warm-up, shower, and so on.) On single practice days, workouts usually last close to 90 to 105 minutes.

I also help wrestlers get ready for specific opponents through one-on-one coaching sessions before, during, or after practice. Don't get caught up in what your team's opponents do as compared to what your athletes are going to execute. Too much video time watching opponents can cause mental blocks. Watching himself execute and win can boost a wrestler's level of confidence more than studying his opponents. Knowing an opponent's tendencies is good, but don't dwell on them.

Tournament Time

If you have a large enough facility and enough people on your coaching staff, this is the ideal time for individual training. Sometimes teammates can help with the coaching or at least monitor their peers' practice performance.

A typical time frame for an individual practice would be:

1. Warm up for 15 to 20 minutes.
2. Combative wrestling and preparing for individual or specific situations for 5 to 10 minutes.
3. Combative wrestling with aggressiveness and domination as the goals, by using several short 20 second goes with the team representative being the aggressor and his opponent protecting a lead, for 15 to 20 minutes. During this time period do escapes in a similar format. If training freestyle or Greco-Roman, use the top position instead of escapes.

After the combative phase, go immediately into short, explosive conditioning bursts, involving sprinting or a similar apparatus. Depending on how the wrestlers look and feel, have them do 7 to 20 bursts of 10 to 15 seconds' duration each. You might also want to add a couple of rope climbs or chin-ups to finish.

If what you want to take place isn't happening, make immediate adjustments to assure a positive practice takes place. Monitor everything a little closer now to help keep everything in its proper place. Like during the late-season phase, it's more important to be ready to compete than to have a workout risk wrestlers' health. Keep the risk factor to a minimum during this time period.

While planning details for this time period, allow for the unexpected. Give yourself plenty of time, whether it be to work on special areas or to travel for a competition. I always try to plan a detailed program for the final month of training and competitions as far as details and intensity are concerned. This time of year requires adjustments to your personal schedule and focus.

When already on schedule, the following final month of training graph (see pages 77–79) can be very effective for peaking your wrestlers to their maximum performances. It's essential to read them at every practice and be able to make any necessary adjustments.

Your athletes must be able to capitalize on the opportunities they have and not let them slip by. Win or lose here—at least they were ready. And when ready, success often follows.

SUMMARY

Knowing your subject matter is important, but knowing your subjects and their wrestling traits rates right alongside the subject matter. With this philosophy, early season practices will be more productive.

Charting your wrestling team members based on what they have and don't have from the seven essential ingredients helps both the coaching staff and the athlete. These seven essentials are standing wrestling, underneath, strength, conditioning, flexibility, nutrition, and attitude.

Remember, the most important facet of coaching is actual practice time with the team and the more productive the better. One should divide the season into parts to help emphasize what is needed at that particular time. One also should actually break down individual practice sessions to be able to accomplish specific goals daily. With distinct season divisions and with daily practice essentials, business seems to be good on the wrestling mat.

Preparation Plan for the Final Month

Practice Activities

1   Combative wrestling

2   Combative wrestling with no dangerous moves—hand fighting

3   Execution of holds—live drilling

4   Position wrestling—combative and passive

5   Instructional drilling

6   Special tactics/techniques in standing, top, and bottom positions

7   Tactics/techniques involving opponents—teams and individuals

8   Individual workouts involving scoring, explosion, and domination

9   Running conditioning—hard (h) and sprints (s)

10   Strength—circuit (c) and heavy (h)

11   Sauna/massage/relaxation/weight and medical check

12   *Special training and motivational films (t)

* Training films involve the studying of personal and opponents' video tapes.

The chart on pages 78–79 doesn't include the warm-up, discussion, or business-related segments of practice.

All time is measured in minutes.

Number in parentheses indicates number of workouts in day.

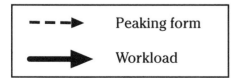

- - - →   Peaking form

——→   Workload

Practice Activity	27 (2) am	27 (2) pm	26 (2) am	26 (2) pm	25 (1) am	25 (1) pm	24 (1) am	24 (1) pm	23 (2) am	23 (2) pm	22	21 (1) am	21 (1) pm	20 (2) am	20 (2) pm	19 (1) am	19 (1) pm	18 (1) am	18 (1) pm	17 (1) am	17 (1) pm	16	15
1		25		25							REST	30		15		15						REST	COMPETITION
2			3	3										5		5				15d 10h			
3		10	5	5	3		3							5		5		20					
4		10		5										5		5							
5		10																					
6				15												5							
7				15												5							
8					35		30																
9				5 h		10 h,s		7 h,s	30 h,s			5 h	20 h,s			10 h					5 s		
10				5 c						45 h						15 c							
11					Weight & medical check		Weight & medical check												120 Weight	Weight & medical check		60 Weight	
12	20 t											30	15 t										

Days

Highest workload

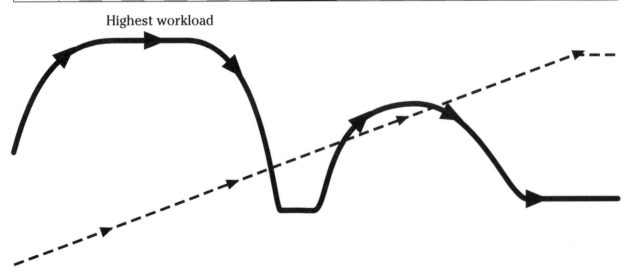

78

Days

	14	13	12 (2)	11 (2)	10 (1)	9 (1)	8 (1)	7 (1)	6 (2)	5 (1)	4 (1)	3	2	1
am pm	am pm	am pm	am pm	am pm	am pm	am pm	am pm	am pm	am pm	am pm	am pm	am pm	am pm	am pm
	C O M P E T I T I O N	R E S T	15	20			R E S T			15	R E S T	C O M P E T I T I O N		
				5						10				
				5				15	3	10				
				5				10	3					
			15											
			20											
			40											
					30	25								
			10 h / 22 h,s	5 h	10 s	5 s				5 s				
							40 h							
					Weight & medical check	Weight & medical check		90 Weight	15	Weight & medical check	60 Weight			
		30 t						45	15 t					

Second-highest peak   Highest peak

Lowest workload

Part III

COACHING SKILLS AND TACTICS

Chapter
7

TEACHING FOLKSTYLE SKILLS AND DRILLS

Because wrestling gets very little television exposure, those of us in the sport must educate and excite young athletes about it. Trying to teach them techniques without first building up their enthusiasm to learn can make coaching more difficult. Get them to attend a few matches, and make sure the environment at the matches is electrifying. Large and loud crowds, entertaining pre-match introductions, P.A. announcing, intense competition, special performances, and supportive coaching all help to motivate prospective wrestlers to join the team and learn the skills needed to be successful.

Perhaps the single most effective thing a coach can do to get the attention and interest of prospective wrestlers for his program is to promote an aggressive, entertaining style of wrestling. Watching an athlete have his way with his opponent in a very physical match can inspire an athlete to learn more. A fired-up student is more likely to study and stick with it.

Before you start teaching specific skills, you need to give wrestlers a basic understanding of the fundamentals of the sport. What are the objectives? What are the rules and how are matches scored? What are the key requirements for success? What are the expectations for physical conditioning? These and more questions will have already been taught if you have a good feeder system with solid coaching at the lower levels.

SEQUENCE FOR TEACHING SKILLS AND DRILLS

One aspect of the sport that surprises inexperienced and poorly taught wrestlers is the importance of body control. That's where I usually begin my instruction. To teach drills and skills properly, you should follow a specific sequence. The following seven-step sequence is good for teaching skills, drills, and other important movements and exercises.

1. Provide a motivational learning situation where all athletes can clearly observe and hear you. If you can include video action footage to support your teaching, that's great!

2. Perform the skill, drill, or exercise several times, showing different angles and repeating key points.

3. Demonstrate the skill with a partner who provides a semi-passive opposition. Repeat it several times.

4. Break down the skill into segments, preferably into no more than three or four phases or steps.

5. Verbally instruct team members through each phase of the skill until they understand them well.

6. Perform the whole skill once or twice more, piecing together the phases or segments of the skill just shown and explained.

7. Have each athlete on the team perform the technique on his own, first in segments, and then as one whole integrated movement.

When teaching skills, drills, or techniques, you need to demonstrate the action first in a tough-passive manner. The demonstrator hits the techniques as he would in a match situation, and the partner provides little resistance. You can demonstrate the technique yourself or have others demonstrate the technique while you do the explaining. During this type of demonstration, add an extra foam gymnastics-type mat to cushion the fall of the passive wrestler on some movements. You can use videotape to substitute for, supplement, or complement the live demonstration.

After you've demonstrated the move or drill several times and learners have the idea of what they are trying to accomplish, break it down into segments. Number the phases or segments of the technique—the fewer the better. When you think the athletes have a pretty good grasp of what you've taught them, put all the numbered segments back together into one maneuver.

During practice after learning a technique or drill, encourage wrestlers to execute the technique or motion in its entirety to eliminate countering by the opponent. A safety rule of thumb is always make the executor of the move the one responsible for making sure people don't crash into others or the wall. The executor should be the one with the vision field to help prevent dangerous events.

When the move is learned and can be performed all in one segment, it still is not an accomplished move. Only when the move is executed under live (tough-tough) conditions will the wrestler get the real feel of it, and total learning will have taken place. Once a wrestler executes a move under match-like conditions, he has a better understanding of it, and the chances are good that he will be able to repeat it when needed. I'm still talking practice, and chances are that's when proper execution of a move will and should first happen. Using the move for the first time is even more difficult to do in a match, but once a wrestler uses a new move successfully in a match, you can look for it to start popping up more often.

GYMNASTIC MOVEMENTS AND TUMBLING DRILLS

Chances are good that your wrestlers have probably had informal, rough-house wrestling matches with brothers and friends since the very early years of their lives. Although these unstructured, unrefereed matches usually produce more rug burns and broken pieces of furniture than they do sound wrestling techniques, they do at least get kids used to the physical side of wrestling and are a normal part of growing up to be a wrestler or to be somewhat competitive. Wrestling is basically a natural form of movement that comes easier when certain exercises and drills are taught first.

What a coach of middle school or high school wrestlers must do is to take their athletes from this "natural" form of wrestling to the structured, competitive wrestling style. Teaching body control is an important prelude to live combative wrestling or performing even the basic drills, techniques, and tactics. The following gymnastic, tumbling type of exercises should be taught and learned before an athlete begins to wrestle competitively. Even more experienced, elite wrestlers will find practicing these moves beneficial.

Many of the movements involve actions similar to those used during a wrestling match. Use these exercises and movements to help with warm-ups, body control, flexibility, conditioning, drills, skills, and cool-downs:

- Jogging and skipping
- Jogging and skipping with arms swinging and high-knee kicking
- Forward rolls
- Army crawls
- Shoulder rolls
- Backward rolls
- Circles while jogging
- Cartwheels
- Figure-eights
- Bridging (see figure 7.1)

KEY FUNDAMENTAL DRILLS

Doing drills that simulate wrestling matches can aid the overall learning process, making the athlete all the more prepared when you introduce more advanced, competitive moves. I won't explain the following drills in-depth, for that is not the purpose of this book. What's important here is to understand which drills are essential, what contribution they make to developing wrestlers, and when they are most effectively used during a workout and season.

Figure 7.1   Starting out in a normal front or back bridge (a) one does a complete 360° rotation (b–c) without moving one's head.

Pummeling Drills

Instead of using combative wrestling during practices close to competition, use pummeling drills (figure 7.2). They're a great substitute for and simulation of live wrestling because they present far fewer dangerous situations. Pummeling drills should be performed in both Greco-Roman and European stances. These hand-fighting drills accomplish several objectives. The main one is that they teach athletes how to move their opponents around so that they can control them and create scoring opportunities. Another objective of pummeling drills is to learn inside position and control. Inside control leads to great offensive scoring opportunities, which means pummeling drills are great set-ups for takedowns.

These drills also complement stance and movement drills and are great for practicing the head and hand positioning that lead to defensive scoring. Pummeling is also great for warm-ups and for late-practice conditioning when everyone is tired, as they can be late in matches. No leg attacking or actual throws are used during these drills. Tie-ups are also mastered during hand-fighting drills. A wrestler should also learn how to move his opponent from these different ties. Positioning yourself well is a key factor in wrestling, and good positioning in hand-fighting drills really helps develop this skill.

Figure 7.2 Both wrestlers in an upright, bent-knee stance alternate inside arm motion back and forth.

Sumo Drill

Another good drill involving pummeling and hand fighting is the Sumo drill (figure 7.3). Each wrestler starts in the middle of a 10-foot practice circle and attempts to maneuver the opponent out of the circle. Both of the opponent's feet have to be out of the circle for it to count. The other way to win is to snap the opponent to the mat while pushing. This drill is great for backing your opponent up or snapping them to the mat. It also helps wrestlers learn controlled penetration from the feet. The first wrestler to force his opponent out of the circle 10 times (or whatever number you choose) wins the drill. No throws or leg attacks are used in this drill.

Figure 7.3   Staying in the upright bent-knee position, both wrestlers try to push both feet of the opponent out of the circle. Snapping to the mat to both knees is also a victory.

Stance, Motion, and Penetration Drills

Stance, motion, and penetration drills (figure 7.4) are another great series of drills for warming up, conditioning, setting up takedowns, and scrambling for position off flurries. They can be done early in practice for a warm-up or late in practice with more intensity for conditioning. Also, if an athlete is fairly beat up and wants to get his body more ready for competition, these drills are good because of their less combative nature.

Figure 7.4   A good bent-knee stance with motion involved (*a*) can be accompanied with an even lower level motion (*b*) when defensing an opponent's shot (*c*).

Level changing (figure 7.5)

Figure 7.5 An outside forehead-to-forehead stance *(a)* can be quickly changed by simply changing levels *(b)*, thus creating an opportunity to penetrate and score.

A good workout the day before competition would be a thorough warm-up (15 to 20 minutes), tough-passive position and execution drilling (10 to 15 minutes), 6 to 8 minutes of live hand fighting, and then 12 short sprints of 20 to 30 yards to finish the workout. A variation of this workout would be to substitute stance, motion, and penetration drills for the 12 sprints run at the very end of practice. Or you might substitute the hand-fighting drills for motion and penetration drills if moves from the outside are key attacks for your wrestlers.

Hip Heist Drills

Many of the stance and motion drills involve hip movements. Hip heist drills (figure 7.6) and moves are closely associated with mat-escaping techniques in wrestling, but they are also tied with movements in all wrestling positions (top, bottom, and so on). The most common moves linked with hip heisting are switches, sit-outs, and rolls. These movements are also used in many different wrestling maneuvers, especially in countering and scoring from the defensive position from the feet.

Figure 7.6   Escaping and flurrying for position happens a lot with these movements *(a–b)*. Being able to move and adjust one's hips without changing mat locations can be a key in successful wrestling.

Leg Attack Finish Drills

The drills in this section are almost a form of football tackling. Leg-attack takedown finishing drills require minimum learning to execute. Use an extra foam mat (crash pad) for these drills to encourage more driving, lifting, and penetrating finishing moves.

Lifting and bringing to mat from feet, with head inside on high single (figure 7.7)

Figure 7.7   With opponent's ankle lifted into the air (a), one's near leg sweeps opponent off his feet (b).

Leg Attack Finish Drills

Driving and dumping from feet, with head inside (figure 7.8)

Figure 7.8 With hips under and head up but tucked across *(a)*, lift and drive at the knee to take the opponent off his feet *(b)*.

Driving and dumping from feet, with head outside (figure 7.9)

Figure 7.9   With hips under and head tight *(a)*, one drives into his opponent while pulling down at the knee and covering across on far side *(b)*.

Leg Attack Finish Drills

Double leg finish (figure 7.10)

Figure 7.10 After lifting opponent off his feet on a double-leg *(a)*, one reaches inside the legs and swings opponent to the mat while dropping to one knee *(b)*.

Sweep—single finish (figure 7.11)

Figure 7.11 While single sweeping opponent's lower leg *(a)*, one comes all the way behind, switches hands while posting *(b)*, drives forward, and post arm grasps opponent's far knee *(c)*.

Leg Attack Finish Drills

Clearing—leg finish (figure 7.12)

Figure 7.12 While attempting a low sweep single, one lifts opponent off the mat, hips under (a). Immediately push far knee over head (b) and drive to a finish at opponent's knees (c).

Low single—lift finish (figure 7.13)

Figure 7.13 Cup the heel while your head is penetrating through on the inside of the knee *(a)*. One swings and lifts *(b)* before pivoting and circling to the feet for the finishing touches *(c)*.

Leg Attack Finish Drills

Low single—sweep across finish (figure 7.14)

Figure 7.14 Use a similar start as the previous lifting technique *(a)*, except that opponent's weight is not dropped over, but instead goes backward. Circling to the far knee and driving works well *(b)*.

Snapdown, Go-Behind Drills

A good philosophy on scoring is that offensive scoring is the first choice, but defense turned to offensive scoring is the second choice. These drills combine both philosophies. Whereas snapping can lead to offensive scoring, countering someone's shots can lead to defense-turned-to-offense scoring. These are the two main moves to practice in these drills.

Snapping and going behind, with opponent on knees (figure 7.15)

Figure 7.15   With opponent leaning heavily into partner *(a)* grasp elbows and lead with hands and wrists in snapping opponent's forearms to the mat *(b).* Other ties such as the collar and inside tie also work well here.

Snapdown, Go-Behind Drills

Snapping from feet (figure 7.16)

Figure 7.16   This is a similar action as in figure 7.15 except it is done from the feet *(a–b)*. Of course the follow-up is a go-behind to score or whipovers can also be generated here.

Opponent shooting and going behind (figure 7.17)

Figure 7.17   Here the go-behind is off an opponent's shot *(a)*. The key is to keep opponent's arm from reaching up and blocking. Weight must be applied to the go-behind side *(b)* as well as creating an angle.

Takedown Machine Drills

The Adam takedown machine helps wrestlers practice leg attacks, set-ups, and penetration (figure 7.18). They can also perform finishes by double hitting to make sure the opponent is going down. Adam also helps wrestlers learn moves after penetration, such as duck-unders. This machine can help wrestlers practice tie-ups and outside motion to penetration as well. Adam is also good for doing warm-ups, drilling without a partner, and practicing when injured.

Figure 7.18 One of the many functions of this machine is to use it to practice set-ups for takedowns. Here, the wrestler is snapping head and shoulder of machine to get it to react (spring-loaded).

Riding and Pinning Drills

As long as there is pinning and, in college, a point for an extra minute of riding time, your wrestlers will benefit from performing riding drills such as the jam drill (figure 7.19). These drills teach control, and wrestlers can use the skills they learn from these drills to tire out their opponents, which can lead to breaking them mentally. Many people argue against the point for riding time, but without this control skill, there would be even fewer pins. The importance of learning moves for pinning an opponent should be obvious. In junior high and high school, more riding is allowed as compared to college where the top person will be penalized quicker. Even though in college there is a point awarded for an extra minute of control, the top person must be working for the pin faster.

Figure 7.19 Off the initial whistle the top wrestler can jam the bottom wrestler forward which helps throw off their movement (hold). Staying behind the arms is key here as well as a repeated jamming action, if necessary.

Near wrist ride drill (figure 7.20)

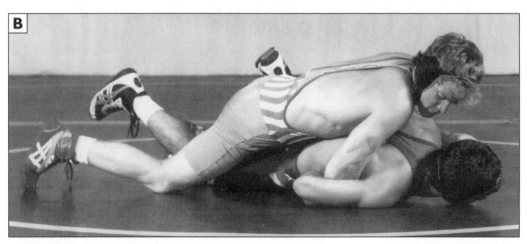

Figure 7.20 Trapping an opponent's near arm and wrist *(a)* can happen when they are base building or can be initiated after jamming. Driving foreword helps trap the wrist *(b)* and circling will keep it there *(c)*.

Riding and Pinning Drills

Leg in—elbow lift drill (figure 7.21)

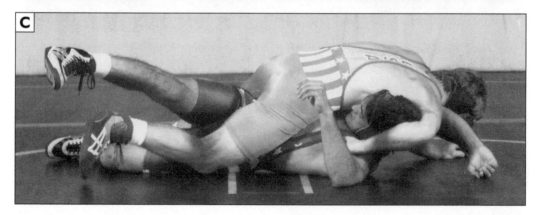

Figure 7.21   Burning your heel in an opponent's thigh while putting chest weight high on their head will isolate the arm needed for trapping *(a)*. Arching up while rotating and sinking a deep half *(b)* will end one in a tight pinning position *(c)*.

Leg switch drill (figure 7.22)

Figure 7.22   With power leg in and arched (a) hold until the other leg replaces (b) and repeat.

Escaping and Reversing Drills

Escaping and reversing drills are another "must learn" area of wrestling for they are one of three key areas for successful wrestling along with offense and defense on the feet. The drills mentioned earlier concerning hip heisting are used here. They can be effective when countering legs in a high-leg over drill (figure 7.23).

Figure 7.23   With top person's leg in *(a)*, bottom person pushes back and hips under *(b)* isolating an opponent's mid-section on the mat. Top (high) leg swings over *(c)* to gain control and a possible reversal or near-fall situation develops *(d)*.

Mat Hand-Fighting Drill

The mat hand-fighting drill involves fighting the top man's hand control as well as digging for the inside position while in the bottom position, especially with use of the elbows. If the top man gets over the other wrestler's arms, that wrestler should be out, especially if the top man combines that control with hip heisting.

Base-Building Drills

Base-building drills are a must for keeping position and balance while flurrying or executing bottom skills.

Unhooking Ankles Drills

Unhooking ankles drills require getting the lower leg free to be able to execute a bottom move from either the opponent's hand grasp as shown in the post drill (figure 7.24) or leg hook at the ankle as in the clearing ankle drill (figure 7.25). Remember, initiating action is better than always fighting action, so hopefully your wrestlers won't have to use the skills from these drills in matches. In most cases, a wrestler's goal should be to not give opponents anything to work with.

Figure 7.24   While opponent grasps ankle *(a)* bottom person pushes back and rolls up onto the foot. At the same time, controlling the top person's hand and wrist while freeing the ankle is necessary *(b)*. Alternate sides back and forth for effective learning.

Figure 7.25   Opponent rides (hooks) ankle of the bottom wrestler with inside leg *(a)*. Bottom wrestler's hips are back and in while sliding hooked ankle out to a hip heist position *(b)*. Note that finishing here with the sit-out and elbow through would free the bottom wrestler for an escape.

Execution Drills

In execution drills, one wrestler performs moves full speed while an opponent offers only modest competition or resistance (tough-passive). These drills are a good final warm-up and great at the end of practice when wrestlers are tired, especially if a wrestler has not performed a lot of techniques during that practice. Switch partner roles every six to eight repetitions to give each wrestler an equal chance to perform the moves and stay focused while doing it. These execution drills are also great (along with pummeling) for pre-competition warm-ups.

Late in the season, this kind of drilling promotes peaking and helps prevent injuries. Stress live execution with set-up, penetration, and the finish coming all in one motion. One helpful hint includes having the partner recover quickly and push back if he's on his feet. If the wrestler is executing on the mat, simple hustle will help with this drill. Also, this type of drilling is excellent for the bottom man to practice his folkstyle maneuvers and great for the top man in freestyle or Greco-Roman wrestling.

Throwing Drills

When performing throwing drills with a partner, using an extra foam mat for landing is helpful. When wrestlers use a throwing dummy (figure 7.26), emphasize going all-out on throws. Lifting and throwing drills are meant for learning throwing skills, but they can also be used for conditioning purposes. Be extra careful where the dummies are landing for safety reasons. The arm throw drill (see chapter 8) is an excellent drill as well. Having a partner to help pick up the dummy will speed up the arm throw drill.

Figure 7.26 Wrestler uses a back-arch movement combined with turning to his base for the follow-through. Repeat several times for conditioning and drilling sequence (six to eight reps). Note that once the drill starts hands should be kept locked throughout the entire exercise.

Back-Step Drill

Like many of the drills and movements presented in this chapter, the back-step drill can be performed by a single wrestler (figure 7.27). The drill involves an action helpful for throwing and should be practiced repeatedly.

Figure 7.27 The wrestler initiating the back-step drill uses a forearm and collar tie and steps across *(a)*. The back foot pivots in *(b)* and hips lower as one pulls opponent's head down *(c)*. Repeat for drill.

Solo Drills

A wrestler has no excuse for failing to work on his skills through repeated drilling. All he needs is the motivation and some helpful instruction and feedback from a coach every now and then. When directly relating these solo drills, a wrestler must use his imagination somewhat to make the drills even more realistic for maximum gains. The following drills are especially good for practices when a partner is not available:

- Stance and motion drills (hand and body feinting and level changing)
- Hip heist drills (switches and sit-outs)
- Bridging drills
- Dummy throws
- Adam takedown drills
- Back-step drill

These particular drills, when combined with a thorough warm-up and hard conditioning, pro-vide great wrestling workouts, especially when workout partners are hard to come by. They're also good to use when competition is nearing, to help stay sharp and healthy. A good ex-ample of such a workout would be to stretch and warm up with jogging and tumbling exer-cises for 15 to 20 minutes, run or bike hard for another 12 to 15 minutes, and then add solo drills for another 12 to 15 minutes. Sprints, push-ups, sit-ups, chin-ups, or rope climbs are a good finish.

SKILL INSTRUCTION

After you've motivated wrestlers to learn, provided a basic understanding of the sport, introduced and had them practice basic drills, and shown them how to put together a good practice session, it's time to start teaching them the key skills of wrestling. All of the preparation work you've done so far will help athletes to grasp the techniques much quicker. You should have a group of fast learners!

Pete Bush, Iowa NCAA national champion, had some big throws that came in handy at some crucial times.

Teaching Folkstyle Skills

When teaching skills, it always helps to know what skills your team has so you can make sure time is not wasted on skills the wrestlers already know well. It's also important to emphasize the basics needed for the most efficient learning so performances can improve as quickly as possible. Results help develop a good rapport between athletes and coaches.

Techniques When on Feet

The moves made on the feet are probably the most important wrestling moves. A wrestler should spend the bulk of his time perfecting these moves. A good takedown artist can go a long way and score a lot of big points or pins from his feet. Doubles, whizzers, near arm far leg tackles, hip tosses, headlocks, and front headlock counters are shown in the following pages. Many others have been or will be mentioned, but are not included in this section. Techniques on the feet, plus second (follow-up) moves are key moves to teach. Other important basic moves include the duck-under, fireman's carry, ankle-pick, and arm drag. The wrestler who becomes proficient at many of these on-the-feet moves will have a leg up on the competition.

Underhook double (figure 7.28)

Figure 7.28 From an underhook and elbow post tie *(a)*, wrestler penetrates in and across as opponent is taken to the mat *(b)*.

Techniques When on Feet

Step-in double (figure 7.29)

Figure 7.29   Changing levels *(a)*, wrestler reaches and steps in with head in opponent's mid-section and drives opponent to the mat *(b)*.

Whizzer (figure 7.30)

Figure 7.30   Wrestler with overhook and far wrist tie hips into opponent putting opponent in danger. The whizzer is a basic move for countering takedowns or escaping; however, it can only be used for an opponent on his back.

Near arm far leg—head inside (figure 7.31)

Figure 7.31 Wrestler with inside tie and wrist control *(a)* circles opponent's left leg into him while stepping to the outside *(b)* and pivoting opponent to his back *(c)*.

Techniques When on Feet

Hip toss (figure 7.32)

Figure 7.32 With an overhook and underhook, executing wrestler steps in *(a)*

with a back-step *(b)*,

lowers hips *(c)*,

drives to lead knee *(d)*,

and ends in a greater than perpendicular position for control *(e)*.

Headlock (figure 7.33)

Figure 7.33 Using the forearm overhook and collar tie along with the back-step movement *(a)*, one drives to that lead knee *(b)* and ends in a perpendicular or greater position *(c)*.

Techniques When on Feet

Short drag (figure 7.34)

Figure 7.34 Missing on a shot and/or getting front head locked will create this position. Immediately reach up and across to the elbow and above on opponent's front headlock arm (a) and drag by while throwing head under and across to free one's body (b) for the go-behind (c).

Techniques When on Bottom

Moves made on the mat or on the bottom are also keys to success. Practice at this position might have to be more structured; otherwise, your very good wrestlers spend little time on the bottom and don't get the practice they need. Make sure all of your wrestlers work on switching, stand-ups, and sit-outs. Other important on-the-bottom moves include rolls, Granby rolls, and combinations, along with base positions and whizzers which were previously mentioned. If a wrestler can master any or all of these bottom techniques along with being good on his feet, he will be a tough opponent to defeat in any match.

Switch and hip heist (figure 7.35)

Figure 7.35   Leading with one's inside arm, the bottom wrestler hips to the outside (*a*) while reaching back with the outside arm (*b*) and hip heists into a leg tackle (*c*) for a reversal. This sometimes results in an escape instead of the reversal.

Techniques When on Bottom

Stand-up (figure 7.36)

Figure 7.36 Bottom wrestler pushes back *(a)* as inside leg pivots up and inside arm stays tucked *(b)*. Outside arm gains wrist control *(c)* while doing a standing hip heist to face opponent *(d)*.

Sit-outs (figure 7.37)

Figure 7.37 Bottom wrestler pushes back to a sit-out position and digs deep with his elbows for inside position and control *(a)*. Once control is established a short hip-heisting movement *(b)* is added to complete the escape *(c)*.

Techniques When on Top

On-the-top moves are icing on the cake, yet some individuals excel here. High school wrestlers can cause some real damage with these moves. Olympic-style wrestlers need to emphasize this area somewhat more. On-top skills aren't as essential, but they can lead to controlling, pinning, and breaking an opponent. Here are some basic moves from on top, in addition to the riding and pinning drills discussed earlier in this chapter.

Lifting and returning to mat skill. This is a great counter to an opponent's stand-up and can actually be a very effective drill as well (figure 7.38). Continuing to pick up an opponent and returning them to the mat safely each time can wear on them mentally and physically.

Figure 7.38 This drill aids riding and finishing takedowns. Wrestler locks around the hips from behind *(a)*, steps to near side, and pops own hips into opponent while swinging him to the mat *(b)*. Bottom wrestler immediately stands up again. Repeat. Do six to eight reps for drill.

Arm bar-head trap. Next to the near wrist attack, the arm bars are a great control and pin variation. The one shown (figure 7.39) requires good power and leverage but is one of the most effective and safe to use. Royce Alger and Dave Schultz had these mastered; therefore, they got a lot of pins. The key point is to pinpoint the opposite shoulder of the trapped arm so the referee doesn't get involved.

Figure 7.39   Top wrestler arm bars and steps to the far side with shoulder post and chin trapped *(a)*. Top wrestler circles around opponent's head *(b)* ending in a tight pinning lock chest to chest *(c)*.

Techniques When on Top

Arm and leg turking. In addition to arm bars, arm (figure 7.40) and leg (figure 7.41) turking have always been my favorites, especially since they are easy to go into during the finish of standing leg attacks.

Figure 7.40   Top wrestler reaches under near leg and traps far leg while containing near shoulder *(a)*. He next lifts and drives opponent over to his back *(b)*.

Leg turking (figure 7.41)

Figure 7.41   Top wrestler lifts near leg, steps in, and hooks far leg above the knee *(a)*. He next drives opponent over to his back while circling and controlling opponent's head *(b)*.

Pinning is the name of the game in many wrestlers' and wrestling fans' minds, but it is not necessary for quick team gains. Pins do create excitement and boost the team point total, however. Additional on-top techniques include the ankle-ride, blanket-ride, and hooking ankle-ride. Teach and drill these skills to keep your wrestlers on top of the competition.

All of these moves are great to know and to be able to perform. If you want to keep it simple and stress a solid foundation of skills, make sure your wrestlers know leg tackles, go-behinds, stand-ups or sit-outs, and leg counters. Everything else is gravy.

SUMMARY

Teaching wrestling first requires eager students. Promote wrestlers' enthusiasm by adopting an aggressive, fundamentally sound style. Prepare wrestlers for specific drills and skill performance by teaching them basic movements to improve their body control. Then progress to effective use of skill-related drills in practice to develop the building blocks that will form the foundation of wrestling techniques that athletes will use during matches. The method for teaching wrestlers skills and drills follows seven tried-and-true steps (page 84). If you know your stuff and use this instructional method, your wrestlers are sure to learn a lot.

The key drills include the following:

✓ Pummeling drills

✓ Stance, motion, and penetration drills

✓ Hip heist drills

✓ Leg attack finish drills

✓ Snapdown, go-behind drills

✓ Riding and pinning drills

✓ Escaping and reversing drills

✓ Throwing drills

Execution drills are good for warm-up and great for the end of practice when the athletes are tired, as they will be at the end of matches. Imagination drills are good for mastering the mental side of performance, practicing when no partners are available, getting ready for competition, or taking a needed break in regular tough training.

Folkstyle wrestling can best be taught by breaking down the techniques into three categories:

- Techniques when on feet
- Techniques when on bottom
- Techniques when on top

If you make wrestling fun and challenging, and promote learning through sound instructional methods, you'll have a solid, winning program.

Chapter

8

TEACHING FREESTYLE AND GRECO-ROMAN SKILLS

Because folkstyle wrestling is only common in the United States, freestyle and Greco-Roman are often called the international styles of wrestling. Some coaches and wrestlers look at freestyle, Greco-Roman, and folkstyle wrestling as different sports, because of the differences in their scoring, skills, strategy, and drills. My viewpoint is that all three styles are variations of the same sport, wrestling. Many of the wrestling skills required for folkstyle wrestling, which I covered in chapter 7, are also required for freestyle and Greco-Roman wrestling. In this chapter, I'll show you how to use various techniques and tricks in each style to complement your performance in the others.

COMPARING THE WRESTLING STYLES

The term *control* is often used to help understand and characterize folkstyle wrestling. In reality, control is a big factor in all three wrestling styles, but if compared on levels of high control to high risk, there is less control in freestyle and Greco-Roman. The word *risk* is more often used to describe freestyle and Greco-Roman. In fact, *slips* are often called in the two international styles, whereas there is no such thing as a slip in folkstyle. Slips occur when one wrestler achieves a dominant position with very little effort at the other wrestler's risk. When a slip is called, wrestlers are returned to the neutral position, and no points are awarded. Let's look at some of the other similarities and differences among the three styles.

Scoring

Scoring differs among the three styles, as shown in table 8.1. These are the current, standard scoring measures for freestyle, Greco-Roman, and folkstyle wrestling, but because rules change, especially in international-style (freestyle and Greco-Roman) wrestling, be sure to check an updated rules book each season.

The less control concept applies not only to the international styles' riskier moves, but also to the cases in which points are scored without one person ending up with control of the other. Simple exposures of the opponent's back to the mat score points in freestyle and Greco-Roman wrestling. As you might guess, refereeing can become rather subjective because of these less-than-clear-cut scoring opportunities. How is a referee to tell during a maneuver whether the angle of the back to the mat was 89 or 90 degrees, especially when that can mean the difference between a wrestler receiving no points or two points? Simple judgments can play big roles in international scoring.

The edge of the mat is one area of controversy in international wrestling. The wrestler who has dominant control either in bounds or going out of bounds is supposed to score points. The problem here is that what is perceived as dominant control by one official is often different from the perception of another referee. Rules clinics are held to eliminate some of the subjectivity, but it is still sometimes a difficult call.

Escapes can also be very subjectively ruled in international wrestling, as evidenced by referees' inconsistency in making this call. An official may have an image of what an escape looks like, but this image isn't always in agreement with how a wrestler breaks an opponent's grip or hold, which is a legitimate escape. In many cases, neither competitor knows whether the situation scored until they get to see the scoreboard. Sometimes even the scoreboards can be wrong and might not be stopped for correction until after a match is over.

Besides the main mat referee, two other mat judges are positioned on the sides of the mat. All scoring requires at least two of the three scoring personnel to agree. In major world and Olympic events, no referee can officiate a match in which a contestant from the same country is competing. Because officials and athletes often do not speak the same language, verbal communication is difficult, which only adds to the difficulty in scoring in international wrestling.

I've been extremely close to international wrestling since 1967, and even today I have some difficulty in attempting to make calls or score a contest. Folkstyle wrestling seems somewhat easier to score because of more defined situations and less subjective rules.

Table 8.1   Folkstyle vs. Freestyle and Greco-Roman General Scoring

Folkstyle	Freestyle and Greco-Roman
Takedown = 2	Takedown = 1
Escape = 1	Escape = 1 (depends on situation; otherwise, no points)
Reversal = 2	Reversal = 1
Near fall (2–4 second count) = 2	Back exposure = 1
Near fall (5 second count) = 3	Danger = 2 (5 second count plus 1)
Fall (1 second—college, 2 seconds—high school)	Lifts 3, 5
Riding time = 1 (college only)	Fall = less than one second
Points for stalling in folkstyle and cautions in freestyle and Greco-Roman can also be awarded.	

Athletes and coaches have very little control over scoring situations and interpretations in international wrestling. Many wrestlers and their coaches have been removed from the mat area after questioning a scoring ruling. Bluntly put, the officials are in charge, and coaches have little control over any scoring decisions or rule interpretations made during a match.

Terminology

Terms commonly used in freestyle and Greco-Roman wrestling are *passivity* and *caution*. A wrestler who is cited very often for either of these infractions places control of the match in the opponent's or officials' hands. Passivity or caution violations are very subjective calls, but the wrestler who puts himself in a position to have either infraction called probably deserves it and is not wrestling in the true spirit of the rules.

Passivity is similar to stalling in folkstyle, except no points are awarded. The wrestler called for passivity can be put in the bottom of the *par terre* position by his opponent. The opponent can also choose to stay in the standing, neutral position. Although there is no limit to the number of passivity calls a wrestler can receive, the winning wrestler's margin of victory in a tie match may come down to the fewer number of passivity calls given.

Cautions are also to be avoided, and a wrestler who receives three cautions in a match is disqualified. The fact that each caution received results in a point for the opponent is another reason to steer clear of cautions. Cautions are usually called on the edge of the mat when one wrestler flees the mat. These calls sometimes are very subjective as well. Besides losing a point, the opponent again gets the choice of top or neutral position. Fleeing a hold is another infraction and can happen anywhere on the mat and is also worth a point as well as a choice of top position or neutral. Again, check with the most current rule book because major changes in scoring and interpretation occur often in the international styles.

The Mat

Mats used for folkstyle and international styles of wrestling differ in their composition and their markings (figures 8.1 and 8.2). Most international mats are thicker in texture. They also have a zone area that is close

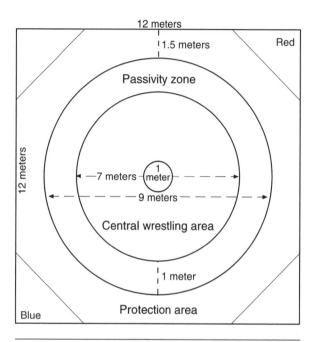

Figure 8.1 International mat

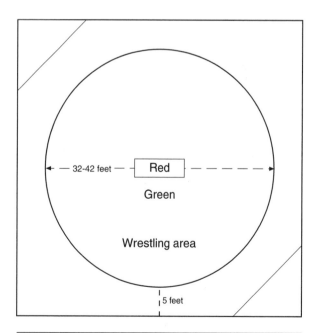

Figure 8.2 NCAA or high school mat, except in high school smaller dimensions (28-foot wrestling area) can be used

to the out-of-bounds line that basically is a warning track saying "get back toward the middle." The center circles are different as well, with the 10-foot center circle being recently eliminated in collegiate wrestling. Since shrinkage occurs in wrestling mats, a minimum of 34 feet is recommended for the in-bounds area. High school mats are the same as NCAA mats except that the minimum in-bounds area is 28 feet.

Timing

Folkstyle time ticks down, letting you know how much time is left; international wrestling time ticks down sometimes and up sometimes, often depending on regulation versus overtime matches. The duration of an international wrestling bout depends on the age category. If neither wrestler has scored three points by the end of a match, another period is added. The overtime ends when either opponent scores three points. Check a current rule book for match lengths of age categories for male and female bouts.

FILA

The International Amateur Wrestling Federation, or FILA, is the ruling body of the sport throughout the world. It oversees all international-style competitions. Like other sports organizations, it's comprised of a bureaucracy of committees that is difficult to penetrate. A democratic ruling is difficult to reach because power in the organization is controlled by a few members who are sometimes in lifetime positions, and who do not always represent the majority.

When the results of matches are contested because of judgment calls, a committee can overturn decisions based on post-match scoring of the videotape. Examples of this power include two matches in the 1995 World Championships held in Atlanta. In the 62 kilogram final, a Japanese wrestler, Wada, was ruled the winner of the match, only to learn an hour later at the awards ceremony that he had lost his title and was dropped to second place. A committee had reviewed his match behind the scenes using video and had reversed the earlier decision. The same thing happened to the American 52-kilogram wrestler, Larry Jones, in an earlier round. This type of controversy—using video to change previous judgment calls—is not allowed by the rules but is done anyway. Video should be used only to rule on objective, nonjudgmental situations, such as incorrect scoring on the clock.

Experienced wrestlers and coaches know that politics and controversial calls are part of the sport because the scoring system isn't as straightforward as putting a ball through a hoop. Even in folkstyle wrestling, mistakes are made in officiating and in interpretation of rules. The key is to focus on performance and not the politics. That's exactly what we'll do in the rest of the chapter.

INTERNATIONAL STYLE SKILLS

Many of the basic skills and drills mentioned in chapter 7 are also used for freestyle and Greco-Roman wrestling. Just as in folkstyle wrestling, you need to establish basic techniques to build a foundation for learning and success. In the two international styles, the quickest way for a wrestler to win is to develop good solid skills in both the standing position and underneath (par terre) position.

In freestyle and Greco-Roman wrestling, it's also especially important to be good in the top position. The reason is that in tight matches, and especially in matches with little or no scoring, both wrestlers could get their chance on top. Chances are this will happen even if one wrestler is more aggressive than the other. In those matches, both wrestlers are given a chance to apply their expertise from all positions.

Freestyle Skills and Drills

Leg attacks are the high-percentage scoring moves for freestyle, but the bottom position requires a learning adjustment from folkstyle. In freestyle, the bottom person's main emphasis is to prevent the top person from exposing his shoulders to the mat, whereas escapes or reversals are stressed in folkstyle. Although the bottom freestyle wrestler can do escapes and reversals, his main tactics would be considered stalling in folkstyle wrestling. The top wrestler has only a short period of time (usually 20 to 30 seconds) to turn the bottom wrestler. If he can't turn or begin turning the opponent, both wrestlers are put back in the standing neutral position.

Folkstyle was my number one priority until college was over. Practicing freestyle wrestling and some Greco-Roman wrestling helped my training in the off-season, however. The variety of styles kept me on the mat more, broke the monotony, and added some new dimensions to my training. When I began wrestling mostly the international styles, I included a little folkstyle wrestling in my training for motivation and variety, as well as for conditioning and practicing escapes.

The ability to scramble, which is required in folkstyle wrestling, gives a folkstyle wrestler an edge in overall positions and in conditioning as compared to the established international wrestler. A wrestler has to learn to be more disciplined in specific areas to really make a great adjustment, however. These areas are bottom defense, a more controlled aggressiveness from the feet while stalking an opponent, and a greater awareness of back exposures from everywhere. Fewer back exposures, even while competing in folkstyle wrestling, reduce the danger of giving an opponent something to work with.

Lastly, because of scoring differences in the folkstyle and international styles, especially on many takedowns (two points in folkstyle and one point in international), freestyle makes you more aware of putting people on their back from basic takedowns. This was another positive of the international style that aided my pinning in my folkstyle wrestling. In addition to the drills presented in chapter 7, the following drills are recommended for developing freestyle and Greco-Roman wrestling technique.

Arm Throw

An arm throw drill is a great standing move for learning to use the step-in or back-step movement (figure 8.3). Besides arm throws, this drill aids headlocks, hip tosses, bear hugs, arm spins, and so on. You should also emphasize the use of dummy throwing, partner throwing, and imaginary drills as well. When the wrestlers have partners, have each wrestler push in and quickly recover and push in again for six to eight repetitions. This drill aids folkstyle wrestling as well. In freestyle and Greco-Roman wrestling, learning this move can earn you three quick points.

Figure 8.3 The executing wrestler forearm ties and underhooks same arm as he steps across *(a)* into a back-step position *(b)* ready to hip pop *(c)* and land perpendicular for control *(d)*.

Gut-Wrench Drills

Gut-wrench drills (figure 8.4) are mostly for freestyle and Greco-Roman wrestling and are used mostly from the par terre position. Different grips and grip locations can be used, but the most common grip seems to be at or just above the hips. Another location is locking high just under the shoulders. This high-gut grip can be combined with a lift to be more effective. A good drill for gut wrenching is to hit a gut one way, then go the other way and repeat. Being able to go either way can be a unique skill that is hard to stop.

Figure 8.4   The top wrestler secures a waist-lock while driving forward *(a)* and exposes bottom wrestler's shoulders while bridging through *(b)*.

Laced Ankle Drills

The laced ankle skill and drill (figure 8.5) and the gut wrench are the most commonly mastered skills. Although used as a mat technique in the top par terre position, the laced ankle can be used efficiently after leg attack positions as well.

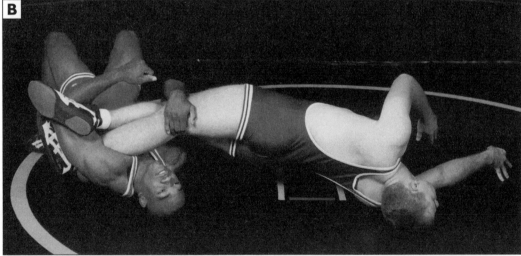

Figure 8.5 Securing both knees and an ankle cross-over grip *(a)*, executing wrestler thrusts into a high bridge roll through *(b)*. Another option is to stand up to turn opponent from same lock.

Lifting and Turking

A wrestler can do this maneuver (figure 8.6) to finish a head-to-outside shot or to counter an opponent's stand-up move. What's impressive about this explosive move is the fact that back points or a pin should be the result. A key for making this lift and turk work is the explosive pop of the wrestler's hips and legs while he lifts the opponent into position to hook legs. 1997 NCAA champion Jessie Whitmer was as good as any with this maneuver; however, three-time NCAA champion Jim Zalesky may have a right to argue this point.

Figure 8.6 Lifting opponent into the air from the front position (*a*) one swings leg in and hooks with own leg (*b*) as opponent hits the mat in the leg-turk position (*c*).

Par Terre (bottom)

This position, like the escape in scholastic wrestling, is a must for doing well. The name par terre is used mostly in freestyle and Greco-Roman wrestling. It means that both wrestlers are wrestling down on the mat, literally *on the ground*. This par terre is often difficult for American wrestlers to adjust to since it is the opposite of attacks normally used in the down position by the bottom wrestler.

Two main defenses are used here if not trying to escape or reverse. Remember, both defenses are used to prevent the top wrestler from exposing the shoulders of the bottom wrestler. Sometimes the bottom wrestler feels the underneath position is for resting and simply waits for the referee to blow him back on his feet. This mentality usually gives the top wrestler an opportunity to score easy points. The bottom wrestler needs to outwork his opponent even in this position. Not conceding any position here is the key, instead of giving position and trying to defense it.

The two most common positions here are the a) prone (lying on the mat and spread out widely) and b) on knees (weight pushed over hips and low to the mat). The two most common defenses to be mastered are the ones that stop the most commonly used offensive turns—defending guts and ankle laces.

Figure 8.7 The defensive (bottom) wrestler spreads "eagle" to keep top opponent from gaining a position of advantage *(a)*. The same objective is used in *(b)*, but from a low base position.

Escapes

The bottom wrestler can move and will be rewarded an escape worth one point in some cases. Any moves the bottom wrestler makes must not expose one's shoulders to the mat; otherwise, the result could be a loss of points. Stand-ups or kick-outs running away from your opponent at the start (with hand control) are good escapes in freestyle or Greco-Roman.

Greco-Roman Skills and Drills

Although legs play an essential role in positioning the body to execute effective Greco-Roman techniques, Greco-Roman wrestling mainly emphasizes effective use of the upper body. Because many leg maneuvers and attacks made in folkstyle and freestyle wrestling are not allowed in Greco-Roman wrestling, lifts and throws are used instead. Throughout a match, lifts and throws from the par terre position are more common than are takedowns followed by lifting or turning. A lift usually adds one extra point to the maneuver.

Greco-Roman is a riskier style of wrestling, because slipping is very common from the feet and from the par terre position. Arm throws, arm drags, duck-unders, hip tossing, and body throws are skills often used from the feet. High-doubles and fireman's carries above the waist are common as well. As a result, using throwing dummies from the standing position and from the par terre position is a very important practice activity for Greco-Roman wrestlers.

Gut wrenching moves made high and at the ribs and hips are common turns of the Greco-Roman style, just as in freestyle wrestling. In Greco-Roman style, a wrestler can step over as a counter to the gut but can't hook legs while doing so. That's why controlling hips on guts is most effective—it prevents step-overs.

Pushing and pummeling drills and changing levels become extremely important in Greco-Roman wrestling. Passivity will be called if no action occurs besides pushing and pummeling and if very little scoring takes place. Positions will be changed back and forth to give each wrestler his chance to show his expertise and scoring ability from the mat position. The aggressive wrestler is supposed to be rewarded and sometimes is, but if no scoring is taking place, both wrestlers will get their chance to score from the par terre position. This happens in freestyle too, but less often.

The wrestler's stance is more upright in Greco-Roman than in other styles, and the par terre position is the basis from which most key points are scored. Wrestlers have fewer scoring options from the standing position in Greco-Roman wrestling because they're not able to attack the legs. However, they have fewer defenses to worry about as well. The following are skills and drills used and practiced for Greco-Roman wrestling, organized according to the position from which they are executed.

Ducks

This drill (or actual move) is a must for being able to score in Greco-Roman. The ability to drop one's hips quickly leads to many scoring opportunities. This drill and scoring move is also a common second move in high school, collegiate, or freestyle wrestling.

From standing (figure 8.8)

Figure 8.8 With head position under and into opponent's diaphragm area *(a),* one commits his hips to a full drop position *(b)* before picking opponent up and returning to the mat.

From mat (figure 8.9)

Figure 8.9   Blocked by an opponent's overhooks *(a)* one creates a quick movement and commits themselves to a deep duck position *(b)* for the go-behind.

Arm Drags

There are several types of arm drags to use. This is one that works well when used effectively (figure 8.10). This arm drag comes from the Russian two-on-one tie.

Figure 8.10   Off a two on one tie the wrestler drags with his inside arm *(a)* while sliding behind the opponent and reaching with far arm for hip control *(b)*. Downward weight helps here.

Front Headlock

This standing front headlock (figure 8.11) is often difficult to get in Greco-Roman because of the upright stance used in that style of wrestling.

Figure 8.11 Wrestler applies the front headlock position from standing *(a)*, and with shoulder pressure downward and, while stretching opponent forward with his head going to the mat *(b)*, looks for the go-behind.

Reverse Lifts

The great Russian wrestler, Alexandr Karelin, perfected this technique (figure 8.12) to the point of having his opponents fear it happening to them. Because of this fear of injury, many would simply roll over for him. Guts and lifts are the two main *scoring* opportunities from the top par terre position.

Figure 8.12   Top wrestler takes a reverse body lock from the par terre position *(a),* hips into a standing position, and swivels opponent around to whatever position he wants *(b).* The drill here would be a 180°-turn back and forth. This lift usually ends with a toss.

Par Terre Bottom Position

The bottom defenses that need to be mastered (see figure 8.7 on page 134) come from learning how to position one's body, making it feel like it's part of the wrestling mat and floor—rock solid and immovable.

SUMMARY

Most of the techniques featured in this book are for folkstyle wrestling. Incorporating skills, drills, and competition in the international styles will help your wrestlers develop a full wrestling repertoire. Differences in freestyle and Greco-Roman philosophy and scoring don't diminish the benefits of learning these two styles.

The best athletes are those who can rise above the politics of the sport, not be discouraged by unfavorable decisions, and push themselves to excel. The more options and resources your wrestlers have for dealing with difficult situations in matches, the better off they will be. This chapter gave you many international style wrestling skills and drills to prepare your wrestlers as much as possible. Even if your wrestlers compete only in folkstyle competition, make time to practice freestyle and Greco-Roman techniques and tactics through the drills provided in this chapter. If you do, your wrestlers will be more solid and more versatile on the mat—and tougher to beat.

Chapter 9

DEVELOPING ADVANCED WRESTLING SKILLS

Once an individual wrestler or a team reaches a new level of performance, it's time to climb another rung of the wrestling ladder. That's the challenge of sports: never be satisfied with your present status. Keep working toward the highest level of excellence you can possibly achieve. Continually strive to keep interest and motivation high and to teach and develop skills long after the basics have been mastered. The same old thing leads to plateaus and to failure. Reaching new levels requires variety, additions, adjustments, and improvements.

ADDING TO THE PACKAGE

An easy way to make progress is to take the already learned skills and add a variation to them; a new finish or set-up off a single-leg situation is just one example. Such additions expand an athlete's skills as well as heighten his interest. If a wrestler stays in the sport long enough, somewhere along the line he'll need every technique you can teach him.

In the United States, we use all three wrestling styles (folkstyle, freestyle, and Greco-Roman) and therefore can select a variety of skills from the other two styles to enhance performance in the primary style. Using other styles can add to the total learning process, yet many feel it hampers Americans' international performances. These people claim that using other styles interferes with style-specific training time and skill development. In my personal experience, the different styles aided my progress in wrestling because they increased the amount of time I spent training. The variety added interest and created more opportunities to compete and learn many skills, which I may not have had in a one-style system.

Attacking From Every Angle

Besides taking techniques that have already been learned and adding another set-up or finish, you can teach wrestlers to apply their already established skills to the opposite side of the body. Ultimately, you want to develop the ability to attack both sides and as well the lower and upper parts of the body and to be able to do so on the feet and from the top and bottom positions. How can an opponent prepare for or defend against a wrestler who is so versatile in his attack position and angle?

To reach the upper echelon of wrestling, an athlete needs to be able to have at least one dependable attack for both sides and hopefully in all three major positions. At

minimum in folkstyle, a wrestler must be able to attack from the standing and bottom positions. In freestyle and Greco-Roman wrestling, you have to include the top position as well.

Adding to Technical Skills

To improve wrestling skills beyond a basic point, you can add variety to previously established holds. You can also teach more complex skills, but those usually take longer to master because typically a completely new position has to be learned. Although the majority of wrestlers have a hard enough time handling and executing a minimum number of skills, even they should be exposed to and attempt new and challenging techniques. Placed in the right practice situations and provided enough successful experiences by their coaches, these athletes will stay hungry and work hard to expand their skills.

These new skills come from many different places. They can be learned from competing

Mike Uker, two-time Iowa NCAA All-American, enrolled in the Greco-Roman development program at the USOC to further his wrestling after college. Here Mike uses his talents to put himself into position for success.

A Timeline of Valuable Challenges

Youngsters often start wrestling when they're in junior high. Fortunately, the Waterloo YMCA offered a program for 5th and 6th graders, and I participated the first year I was eligible. No competitions were held; it was strictly a learning and practice situation. In the 6th grade, I sometimes practiced with the junior high (7th to 9th grade) kids. When I was in junior high, I sometimes practiced with the high schoolers.

In the summers after my sophomore and junior years, I attended a summer wrestling camp. At this time, summer wrestling camps were not as popular or prevalent as they are today (not even close). Throughout my high school career, I was tutored by one of the greatest high school wrestling coaches of all time, West Waterloo's Bob Siddens. His coaching records still stand.

In the summer after my senior year I was invited to and attended an Olympic developmental camp for freestyle and Greco-Roman wrestling. At this camp, I had the opportunity to wrestle and learn from former world and Olympic champions from Japan, including Yoshiro Uetake, a two-time Olympic freestyle champion and Ichiguchi, an Olympic champion in Greco-Roman wrestling. At this camp, I also watched films of Japan's Watanabe who ended his career with 187 wins and no losses. He is considered one of the greatest wrestlers of all time.

Going to college at Iowa State was my next good move; there I learned a great deal from the famous coaching legend, Dr. Harold Nichols. Freshmen were not eligible by NCAA restrictions, but I did compete unattached in several important tournaments during my freshman year. In the summer after my freshman year, I attended the U.S. Pan American Training Camp as a workout partner, thanks to a friend, Bob Buzzard. In 1968, I attended the Olympic training camp for one month in Alamosa, Colorado. In 1969, besides competing for ISU, I wrestled in the National Freestyles after the regular season.

In 1970, in addition to wrestling at ISU, I wrestled at the National Freestyles and attended the World Championships in Edmonton, Canada, as an alternate. As I helped prepare the American wrestlers, I also observed many of the foreign wrestlers in their preparation. At this event I learned that I could dominate the competition by having a greater level of intensity and a more physical style of wrestling than the majority of the competitors. It's funny that I learned this by observing and not actually participating. Observation is a very important perspective for getting better and understanding the surroundings.

In 1971, I competed in the Tbilisi tour in the Soviet Union. I also wrestled in the Pan American Games in Cali, Columbia, and competed in the World Championships in Sofia, Bulgaria. In 1972, I made the Tbilisi tour again as well as the Olympic Games in Munich, Germany. During this year, 1972, the Soviet team toured the United States, and I wrestled in all four dual meets during their visit.

In 1973, I started coaching at Iowa as an assistant and helped with the Tbilisi tour as a coach. Besides the Iowa coaching position, the following kept me current:

- 1974: Assistant coach of the World Team in Istanbul, Turkey.
- 1975: Assistant coach of World Championships in Minsk, Soviet Union.
- 1976: Assistant coach of Olympic Games in Montreal, Canada.
- 1977: Started head coaching position at University of Iowa. Head coach of World Team in Lusanne, Switzerland.

- 1978: Head coach of World Team in Mexico City, Mexico.
- 1979: Head coach of World Team in San Diego, California.
- 1980: Head coach of Olympic team that was to compete in Moscow.
- 1981: Assistant coach of World Team in Skopji, Yugoslavia.
- 1982: Attended World Championships in Edmonton, Canada.
- 1983: Attended World Championships in Kiev, Soviet Union (now Ukraine) as head coach.
- 1984: Head coach Tbilisi Tour in Soviet Union and of Olympic team in Los Angeles.
- 1985: Attended World Championships in Budapest.
- 1986: Attended World Championships in Budapest and was head coach for Goodwill Games in USSR.
- 1987: Attended World Championships in France.
- 1988: Assistant coach of Olympic team in Seoul, Korea.
- 1989: Attended World Championships in Switzerland.
- 1990: Attended World Championships in Tokyo.
- 1991: Missed Worlds, but viewed all tapes.
- 1992: Bought TV package that showed all wrestling competitions, watched it live mostly from 2 to 4 a.m. daily.
- 1993: Attended World Championships in Toronto.
- 1994: Head coach for World Championships in Istanbul.
- 1995: Attended World Championships in Atlanta, Georgia.
- 1996: Attended Olympic Games in Atlanta, Georgia.
- 1997: Missed Worlds, but viewed tapes and sent assistant coach Tom Brands as well as having Lincoln McIlravy (volunteer coach) participate.
- 1998: Attended World Cup in Stillwater, Oklahoma; attended Goodwill Games in New York City; and attended World Championshiips in Tehran, Iran.

Besides coaching at Iowa, I have also coached 10 World Cup teams and several foreign (usually United States versus the Soviet Union) dual matches in America. Every year, I order World Championship tapes of all matches, usually both in freestyle and Greco-Roman. I have also attended some Greco-Roman World Championships. I have tapes of every one of my wrestler's performances to view and study. After close evaluation, I am able to share the knowledge obtained from these events with my team and coaches.

---

in high-level wrestling matches, but only elite competitors get exposed to this situation. More likely, such skills are learned through studying the videotapes of the best wrestlers and wrestling teams and individuals, and then trying to take what you've seen from the screen to the mat.

Seeking Learning Opportunities

Throughout my career as a wrestler and wrestling coach, I've been motivated to seek a higher level of understanding and performance in the sport. The experiences I had as a result of this search helped me succeed in

John Oostendorp, two-time NCAA All-American, utilized a development program to enhance his performance in wrestling to a point of actually winning a couple of USA national Greco-Roman titles.

wrestling. These experiences didn't happen by accident. Hard work? You bet. Disappointments along the way? A few. But exposing myself to new challenges is the only way I know how to get the most out of my abilities. If you want to be your best in the sport, put yourself in a position to have those beneficial experiences that will serve to push you to achieve your potential.

To be the best and stay the best requires a lot of homework. Staying current with the best wrestling moves and training techniques is very helpful to you and your coaches and athletes. Getting support people or fans to attend some of these events can help as well. Their resources are invaluable.

Building a Library of Knowledge

Keeping a library of information can help wrestlers and coaches in specific situations. This library is not limited to skills alone, but includes motivational books and information on psychological preparations, nutrition, strength, and flexibility. Besides books, several worthwhile video and audio tapes are available to help with the growing process.

While the Soviet Union and several other countries were having tremendous success in wrestling, I would search out periodicals and books from these countries hoping they were translated into English. Many were not, but the photos or drawings helped to expand my knowledge anyway. I highlighted many of the pages and important points in these books for quick reference when needed.

Many FILA publications are in English and French, and they have publications for all levels of competitors in both freestyle and Greco-Roman wrestling. Also included in these publications are several biographies of former wrestling greats that are enjoyable and inspirational reading. Several of the action photos alone are especially interesting because many of them are showing people I've heard about but never had the chance to watch.

Developing Through Special Programs

During the off-season, wrestlers can get involved with other wrestling programs. For example, freestyle and Greco-Roman tournaments and training camps are available. USA Wrestling offers live-in programs right on the Olympic Training Center sites for the development of certain wrestlers with Olympic potential.

Two of my former wrestlers, Mike Uker and John Oostendorp, have been in the Greco-Roman developmental program. Even though John didn't win an NCAA championship, he has already been to the top of the Greco-Roman program and has represented the United States in World Championship events. Mike is just starting the program and he, like John, was not an NCAA champion.

Using Statistics Carefully

Statistical analyses of wrestling performances can be extremely detailed. USA Wrestling's national coaching personnel put together a thorough statistical sheet on their national team's performers. Statistics for the World Championship and Olympic teams' performances are particularly precise. Bruce Burnett, USA's national coach, spends a lot of time in this area to help prepare for future events. This type of feedback can reveal exactly what is happening during individual matches, but its usefulness to you and your athletes can vary depending on the circumstances.

You can use positive feedback from statistical analysis to motivate your athletes by showing them what they are accomplishing. Sharing a troublesome statistical report with an athlete can hold him back if he develops a fear or mental complex about specific situations. Scrutinize the statistics carefully to determine how best to use them to maximize future performance. Sometimes, a little deception can work wonders and help eliminate the flaws. The key here is to know your athletes and know what forms of evaluation get the best response from them.

Scouting

From a coaching standpoint, you must know the opponent well. Scouting and thinking about an opponent can be done to a fault, however. Some coaches overemphasize the opponent and neglect their own team. If wrestlers are only working to stop their opponents' moves and tactics, they've lost sight of the goal of the sport.

The amount of scouting information given an athlete before a match will depend on each wrestler's makeup. Although wrestlers should be aware of their opponents' strengths and prepare a defense for them, sometimes the best defense is a good, aggressive offense. As the competition gets close, wrestlers should emphasize their own techniques and tactics and simply be aware of the opponents, not be looking out for them. Execution is the name of the game. A strong, strategic, skillful attack will put points on the scoreboard and your opponent on his back.

DEVELOPING ADVANCED SKILLS

Now it's time to go to the next level in performance. Wrestlers need to know and practice these beyond-the-basic skills to move closer toward mastering their opponents. My first national champion, Chris Campbell, was a perfect technique wrestler.

Chris Campbell, two-time NCAA champion, world champion, and Olympic bronze medallist, took almost a decade off from competition. However, he took care of his health during this time and came back to win again in his late thirties.

Sweep Double-Leg Tackle (Standing)

The sweep double-leg tackle (figure 9.1) is a combination of a fake outside single leg and a double cut across at the knees. Finishing this slick move usually requires very little effort because the opponent is faked out by the first part of the move and lands on his butt through a reaction to the rest of the move.

Figure 9.1   The attacking wrestler changes levels and fakes hard to the outside with arm and leg *(a)*. A complete change in sides happens while keeping a hold of far knee and reaching for near knee *(b)*. Follow through with the finish, which is a sliding knee tackle *(c)*.

Of the wrestlers I've coached, the one that hit this move the best was Jim Heffernan (four-time All-American from 1983 to 1987 and national champion). Jim was very good technically. Another athlete who used this move well was Royce Alger (Iowa wrestler from 1984 to 1988). The interesting point here was that Royce was not known so much for his slickness as his power and toughness, yet this advanced skill was part of his repertoire. The message here is to be open-minded in teaching new skills; you never know what might click for someone.

Apparently, Royce Alger *listened* more than one would think, for even though he emphasized power in wrestling, he was able to perform several highly technical skills on the mat.

Dresser Dump (Standing)

The Dresser dump (figure 9.2) is set up from either a front headlock position or from an opponent backing out after their shot. I've had several athletes use this move effectively, most notably Kevin Dresser (Iowa wrestler from 1982 to 1986), for whom this skill is named. He, Chad Zaputil (three-time All-American and three-time Big Ten champion), and Mike Uker (two-time All-American and Iowa wrestler from 1993 to 1997) were three of the best with this skill.

Figure 9.2 Using the arm that controls the head on a front headlock, reach and drive to the cross knee *(a)*. While controlling the overhook arm, let opponent's head slide through as one hits the mat *(b)*.

Cross-Ankle (Standing)

The cross-ankle (figure 9.3) skill is used off the front headlock. When used in combination with the Dresser dump, the cross-ankle move is difficult to stop. The opponent's reaction to each of these skills enables the other wrestler to use the other skill to get the advantage.

Figure 9.3   While controlling the front headlock *(a)* use overhook to reach at and through to cross ankle *(b)* and drive opponent to the mat to a near-fall or pinning situation *(c)*.

Front Headlock-Knee Tap (Neutral Position)

To perform the front headlock-knee tap (figure 9.4), the person with the front headlock arm reaches through with the same arm and blocks the opponent's knee while driving into them, making sure that the shoulder is below as well. This shoulder position gets the penetration needed that will help the skill work. To help this skill be effective, the wrestler should pull the opponent into himself so the needed knee is close. Make sure the wrestlers do not turn the body with the lead arm; otherwise, the short drag counter could be executed against them.

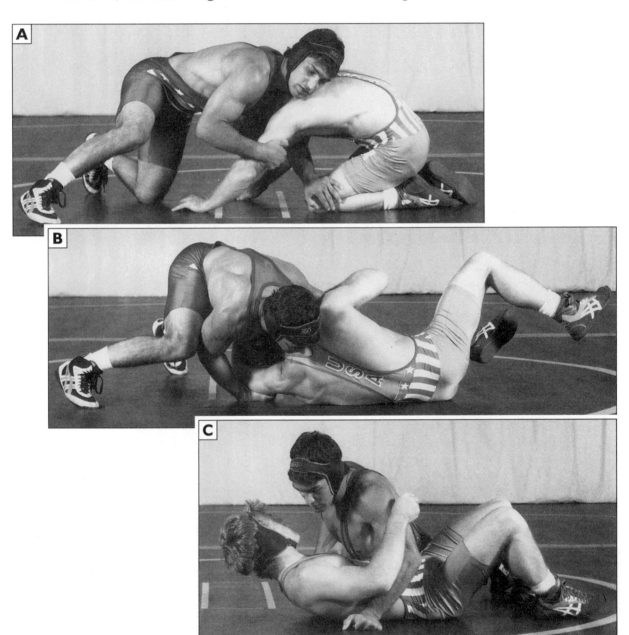

Figure 9.4   From the front-head position on the mat, arm around head reaches across and blocks opponent's knee (a). Pulling on overhook arm and driving in opponent will knock him to his side (b). Follow through by ending in a chest-to-chest pinning situation (c).

Two wrestlers, Royce Alger and Chad Zaputil, used this move very effectively for Iowa. The team named the move "Zap tap" after Chad. Chris Campbell, another former Iowa great (1973 to 1977) and world champion, was superb at this move. This move often puts the opponent directly on his back. Another common reaction is for the opponent to go "belly down"; if this happens, the wrestler should execute a quick go-behind.

Front Headlock Counter

The front headlock counter variation involves grabbing an elbow and setting the front headlock in motion and then reaching through and blocking the knee while doing a Kelly-type move. Bill Zadick (Iowa wrestler from 1992 to 1996, two-time All-American and NCAA champion) and Jim Heffernan were the two wrestlers that executed this counter very effectively.

Standing Head and Knee Tackle

The standing head and knee tackle (figure 9.5) has been used effectively by many but none better than Tom Brands (1988–1992, four-time All-American, three-time NCAA champion, 1993 world champion, and 1996 Olympic champion). Initiating a collar-tie is the start, and getting the opponent to circle his cross leg toward you helps set up this tackle. The free hand hooks the opponent behind his cross knee; driving through then will result in a good scoring move.

Figure 9.5   With a collar and inside tie *(a)* circle opponent into inside tie arm and at the same time block circling leg at the knee *(b)* and drive to the mat covering across opponent *(c)*.

Drag and Trip (Standing)

This maneuver (figure 9.6) became famous when the Soviet Union's three-time Olympic champion Alexander Medved took the United States' bronze medallist (450-pound heavyweight) Chris Taylor off his feet for the winning score in the 1972 Munich Olympics. The drag and trip is a great heavyweight skill, but it can be used successfully at any weight because all the forcible weight is going in the same direction. The drag is used for the set-up that gets the opponent to pull back in the same direction of the executed move. Covering the hips low when hitting the mat is crucial for enough control to stop opponent's counter attacks of redrags or hip heists.

Figure 9.6   With a wrist and cross tie *(a)* one drags arm while stepping his ankle across to block and trip opponent's ankle *(b)*. While completing move here, cover back across hips.

Inside Trip (Standing)

A wrestler must first get his opponent out of a good wrestling stance to correctly execute this driving penetrating move (figure 9.7). The key to completing this move well is to stay parallel and lead with the legs and hips at a low level. Following through with good coverage of the hip and below makes for a good finish. Many have done this move well but none better than former Iowa four-time All-American Joe Melchoire (twice at Iowa and twice at University of Oklahoma before transferring to Iowa) or three-time All-American Royce Alger.

Figure 9.7 With overhook tie and same-side leg stepping inside opponent's legs *(a)*, block opponent's near ankle and drop one's hips down and into opponent *(b)* while covering hips on the mat *(c)*.

Granby Roll and Counter

The Granby skill (figure 9.8) is an effective escape/counter that is used very often during flurries in high school and collegiate wrestling. Steve Hunte (Iowa wrestler from 1974 to 1978, two-time Big Ten champion), Brad Penrith (Iowa wrestler from 1984 to 1988, NCAA champion, three-time All-American), and Steve Martin (Iowa wrestler from 1986 to 1990, All-American) used this series of moves very well during their days at Iowa. Steve's father, Billy Martin, coached high school wrestling at Granby High School (get the connection?). Terry Brands, who had to battle Steve for varsity competition, used the hand post counter action to combat the Granby roll.

Figure 9.8 With bottom wrestler attempting a Granby escape *(a)*, top wrestler pulls out arm around hips and posts by opponent's shoulder *(b)*, while pivoting around to opponent's opposite side *(c)*.

Double Trouble

This skill is a pinning combination off a whizzer, either while an opponent is countering your takedown or is trying to escape from the bottom. The wrestler comes over the top and locks at the armpit (figure 9.9).

Figure 9.9   From an opponent's whizzer position, one reaches and drives opponent's head down while locking under far armpit *(a)*. Continue to drive opponent over to his back while ending chest to chest *(b)*.

Standing Lat Whip-Over

This move (figure 9.10) can be used when countering an opponent's duck-under or while escaping in conjunction with the stand-up. Grabbing a lat and tripping the opponent's close leg can give them lessons in flight school (air time). And again, like the Double Trouble, it can end up in a pinning situation and hopefully a fall.

Figure 9.10   From opponent's rear-standing position, reach back to far lat *(a)* while hipping into and blocking near leg *(b)* and then posting *(c)* as opponent hits the mat.

Leg Sweep

The leg sweep (figure 9.11) works well after an initial leg attack. The opponent pulls up, and the wrestler hits the move with his hips under as he reaches the opponent's upper body. This move often starts from an underhook position. I've had many wrestlers who have executed this move quite well, but the three names that first come to mind are Bud Palmer (Iowa wrestler from 1975 to 1979, two-time All-American), Scott Trizzino (Iowa wrestler from 1977 to 1981, three-time All-American), and Tim Riley (Iowa wrestler from 1980 to 1984, three-time All-American). Royce Alger would be upset if I didn't mention his name with this skill; and, more recently, All-American Kasey Gilliss has hit this skill at appropriate times. Another effective variation of the leg sweep is the two-on-one tie to the near-side leg sweep.

Figure 9.11 From an underhook and elbow tie, one straightens opponent upright and hips into them as well as blocking (sweeping) opponent's underhook-side foot in the air. A good follow-through to the mat is needed.

SUMMARY

Going to a higher level of excellence requires many facets of learning that go beyond the basics:

- Enhance performance by utilizing all the styles of wrestling (folkstyle, freestyle, and Greco-Roman) at appropriate times.
- Practice attacking from all positions and angles.
- Study the great ones and their styles.
- Put yourself in learning situations throughout your career.
- Keep notes, resources, and valuable instructional tools close by; be a student of the sport.
- Use statistics of your team's competitions in positive ways.
- Be aware of your opponents' strengths, but don't let them dictate what you do in competition. Force the action.
- Add to your repertoire of skills and continually work to refine them to always be technically prepared.

Chapter

10

STRIVING FOR PERFECTION

I f you have laid a solid foundation for the program, trained your athletes to a high level of conditioning, and developed advanced skills, you should win consistently. That's enough to satisfy most administrators, fans, and parents, and some athletes and coaches. When high achievers in wrestling reach this point, however, they start asking themselves a few questions:

- What can I do to get to the next level?
- Can I be content where I am or should I try for something more?
- Am I willing to push beyond what I've achieved to what I believe is my full potential?

The greatest athletes and coaches in sports are never completely satisfied with their current performance level or achievements. There's always another hill to climb, a challenge to overcome. Michael Jordan was generally considered the best basketball player ever long before he retired from the game the first time. Still, he continues to refine his game and build even further on his physical and mental strengths. The same is true of Wayne Gretzky in hockey. The best become the best because they are always striving for perfection.

In this chapter, I want you to keep asking yourself "What can I do next to get better?" I've been fortunate because the motivation to improve has never been a problem for me. While other wrestlers and coaches I've known throughout my career seemed to lose their passion for the sport, I've always been able to find a new challenge. If an opponent scored a point, I'd challenge myself to shut him out in the next match. If my team had four first-place finishers, I'd strive for five or more champions next time. Competing was the process; dominating was the goal.

You can add a new skill or tactic. You can improve some aspect of your training program. You can become a more serious student of the sport. You can work on the mental side of your approach. You can be an even better manager of your time. The number of new challenges in wrestling are limited only by your own drive to excel.

Doing What It Takes

In 1975 I was teaching at a wrestling camp in Adrian, MI when I got a call from a friend of mine who was still actively competing. He asked me if he could drive in for a workout with me. I said yes, figuring he was in the local vicinity. I came to find out he drove in from three hours away, had a wrestling workout with me for a couple of hours, and then drove back home. This is the kind of determination that is needed for success.

The wrestler's name is Stan Dziedzic, Olympic bronze medallist in 1976 and world champion in 1977. Determination of this kind is hard to find, but it pays off. Stan, being determined, wanted to train with me, knowing he would get a great workout. He was willing to do so at the expense of traveling six hours to get one good workout. The workout was tough on him, which is exactly what he was looking for—learning how to battle.

PERFECTING THE GAME PLAN

Sit down and map out how to get to this new, higher level of expertise. Analyze all facets of your program and see where improvements can be made. Something can be improved in all areas, even if you're winning year after year. Little things can make a difference. Looking back on my situation at Iowa, here's what I might have done to upgrade the program:

- Improve staff relations and responsibility by communicating better and having more productive staff meetings.
- Make sure I stayed in closer touch with every athlete without smothering them, keeping notebook or computer records of when I last talked to each team member one-on-one.
- Keep the wrestling exercise equipment cleaned and well maintained so that it was always ready for use and working well.
- Revise the schedule to include more conference schools and make sure the top teams visited Carver-Hawkeye Arena yearly.
- Keep my office cleaner and more organized. Set up a system for a more efficient flow of paperwork.
- Increase my involvement in USA Wrestling to improve my level of expertise and communication with more of the best wrestlers and coaches in the country and world.

This list could go on and on, but you get the idea. Something always needs working on, whether it be staff, athletes, equipment, techniques, philosophy, or psychology.

Streamlining and Supplementing Skills

Fine-tuning specific wrestling techniques could have been the main focus of this chapter. No wrestler is so perfect technically that he cannot improve. In striving for perfection, always keep skill improvement near the top of the list. Just don't make it the whole list!

One of the best ways to refine technique is to study the great athletes closely and see what they're working on. Chances are they are developing unique techniques to add to their already advanced skill repertoire. For example, the Brands brothers and Lincoln McIlravy were recently working on new varieties of scoring moves from conventional situations. I'll add these to the list of moves other wrestlers might use in similar scoring positions. Even if a move doesn't fit into someone's style, it might be beneficial for motivational purposes.

MASTERING SPECIFIC TACTICS

Each wrestler must understand his own capabilities and learn to wrestle within those parameters. As a coach who stresses a hard-working, dominating style, I must also realize that not everyone fits that mold. As the level of competition increases, wrestlers who've mastered their style and perfected unique moves that best fit within their approach will often rise to the top. Their talent level is high, but what makes them special is how they maximize their ability by developing nearly unstoppable tactics within their well-suited style.

To master the tactics of wrestling, first play the percentages. Consider factors such as body type, rules, and scoring system when deciding what tactical approach to take. Then add an extra 10 minutes a day of technical and tactical work on to your wrestlers' already established regimen. That's a good extra hour per week toward becoming the perfect wrestler!

USING IMAGINATION TO THE FULLEST

Once you've developed a high level of expertise and understanding in a specific subject, learning can happen in ways that most people won't ever understand. Before that stage, observation, explanation, study, and practice are necessary for learning to take place. That's how I learned how to wrestle and how everyone else learns, at least initially. As my understanding and knowledge of wrestling increased over the years, I've been able to envision, sense, and grasp new techniques in other ways. For example, when I see a wrestling move executed on video and review the tech-

nique several times, I can feel it, fully understand it, and place it in my repertoire.

This type of visualization can be very powerful. Visual cues, such as the wrestling move on the video, trigger a set of physical responses because over a lifetime of participation and observation I know how the move would feel. This process can be a great aid to higher level learning of the sport. With practice, I have been able to use this advanced form of visualization for purposes beyond discovering new techniques.

One of the most interesting examples involves visualization done while exercising. Vigorous activity seems to stimulate the visualization process even more. I sometimes imagine that I complete a full wrestling workout while physically I do a 55-minute ride on an exercise bike. Before riding, I stretch for a few minutes and then hop aboard the bike. At a low level of riding, I start my wrestling warm-up, mostly jogging. Within a couple of minutes, I increase my jogging to more of a running pace and at the same time begin pedaling faster on the bike.

I then slow to a jog and stop to do calisthenics. As I visualize performing the calisthenics and jogging in between sets, my workout on the bike adjusts in a corresponding manner. Calisthenics such as somersaults, shoulder rolls, circling, hops, and cartwheels prompt a faster pace for short time periods (5 to 10 seconds). When the calisthenics are finished, I increase my working pace until I break a good sweat.

When I get back on the bike after a brief water break and self-massage, I begin warm-up drills in my mind. The drills include snap drills, execution drills, and hard hand-fighting drills that increase in intensity and last about a total of eight minutes, during which my pedaling rate returns to a high working pace. Next, I imagine a few sprints at high-level intensity and take another short break.

This break, like the other one, lasts about two minutes, and then it's on to tough-live combative wrestling, which puts the bike into high speed, corresponding to hard intermittent bursts of power and explosion. Five or six minutes of this activity and exhaustion is

Double Cross Strategy for Gold

In the '96 Olympics, Kendall Cross faced two major issues. One involved making his weight and recuperating for the event. He needed to carefully map out these processes so that everything went according to schedule. The other factor involved his wrestling strategy. Kendall needed to make sure he wrestled in his strongest position, on top. By implementing the proper strategy, he would have plenty of opportunities to score from his favorite position. Kendall's opponent in the gold medal match was a Canadian team member from the former Soviet Republic of Ukraine. He made a major strategic error by challenging Kendall's strong upper body area and did not have the ability to adjust his tactics to take advantage of Kendall's more susceptible areas. A big three-point move early in the match by Kendall pretty much won him the match and the gold medal.

Wrestling with match tactics in mind can help a wrestler's results. Kendall Cross, Olympic gold medallist, did just that in the 1996 Olympics.

Also at the '96 Olympics, Townsend Saunders adopted a strategy that gave him the best chance of becoming the champion. He slowed down his opponents until they weren't as strong and sharp as they were early in the matches. Late in the contests, when Townsend was still strong, he took it to them quick and hard. Townsend won several matches with his excellent tactics and by being crafty and controlling the tempo. He wound up winning a silver medal, all because he had mastered a tactical approach that suited him best against the competition. In fact, his strategy was near perfect, but because of the *near* it cost him the gold.

Townsend Saunders used mat savvy to win the silver medal at the Atlanta 1996 Olympics.

coming on. Add a sudden-victory overtime takedown and another water break is welcomed. Being the old-timer that I am, I'm tired but can do another go. Come on, gut it out. OK, back on the bike for another wrestling go, maybe just three or four minutes of a good pace with bursts of explosion for scoring. Whew!

I've finished the mat work, and now I'm imagining some hard running at the end of practice. I run two minutes at match pace and then jog. Well, maybe I'd better do some execution because I probably didn't score enough and I need to practice my moves. Maybe two to three sets of six scoring situations will do. Follow that with one minute's worth of hand fighting to help my positioning and set-ups. Now I do 25 conditioning and stance drills where I'm sprawling and stalking.

I finish up with a couple of rope climbs, buddy push-ups, and four-way neck exercises. I then walk around and stretch a little before heading for the sauna (in reality). At this point, I'm totally spent, physically and mentally, just as if I had been through a grueling wrestling workout. Boy, that shower feels good!

To recap, these are the real phases of my workout:

1. Stretching
2. Cycling
3. Water breaks
4. Self-massaging
5. Buddy push-ups without buddy
6. Four-way neck exercises
7. Sauna

These are the imaginary phases of the workout on the bike:

1. Jogging
2. Hard-running
3. Sprinting
4. Somersaults
5. Shoulder rolls
6. Cartwheels
7. Circling
8. Snap drills
9. Execution
10. Hand fighting
11. Combative wrestling
12. Stance drills
13. Rope climbs

These types of workouts may seem strange to you, but they are a great alternative for advanced wrestlers to add variety to off-season training, peak while preventing injury, or nurse an existing injury. For old-timers like myself, it's as close as I can get to a real wrestling workout, and the next morning I feel just as sore as if my body had performed all of the things I imagined doing. The real and imaginary phases can be interchanged depending on availability and what is preferred. When a wrestler's imagination has developed to the point where he can envision and feel the technical, tactical, and physical aspects of performance and training, he has a powerful tool that no opponent can stop. The more high-quality learning experiences he can get to soak up and use as a reference base for crystallizing his visualizations, the better.

THE PERFECT JOURNEY

Having spent this entire chapter talking about striving for perfection, I must admit the painful truth: perfection is never really achieved. Under the highest level of scrutiny, even what appears to be a flawless performance will have its tiny imperfections. A gymnastic floor routine, for example, would never receive a perfect 10 if all of the judges were allowed to study every move in super-slow motion on an enlarged screen.

Knowing that perfection is beyond our grasp makes the pursuit of it no less important in achieving wrestling excellence. Ali, Nicklaus, Jordan, and other all-time great athletes always aimed for that one perfect bout, round, and game. The fact that they always came up short of perfect did nothing to diminish the mastery of their performances. Perfection-seeking needs to be kept in perspective. Only God is perfect, so don't let the pursuit of perfection become a destructive force that leads to obsessive and unhealthy thoughts and behaviors and constant unhappiness.

Every great athlete has fallen short at some point. Great athletes become great because they refuse to let their setbacks derail them from their determined quest to be the best. I lost one match my whole college career. It was a devastating blow to my psyche and hurt terribly. My alternatives at that point were to (a) let the loss consume me and spit me out into the ranks of the mainstream or (b) become even more focused on correcting the flaws that allowed the loss to happen and seeing to it that it never happened again. Obviously, *b* was my choice, and I never had to give it a second thought once I was able to refocus. The commitment to do whatever it took in the way of practice, study, training, and mental preparation in order to become the "perfect" wrestler had again been made, and was now even more defined.

SUMMARY

Reaching the highest level of expertise oftentimes takes a career or lifetime of learning. Although you might produce great results at various points along the way, you can always improve. Keep these thoughts in mind as you strive for perfection:

- **Study the best.** They are models from which to learn, if not imitate.
- **Understand your strengths and weaknesses.** Develop special tactics that will allow you to use your special talents to their fullest and bolster up the weak areas so opponents have no place of refuge.
- **Extra work always helps.** Building a strong faith in the One Perfect Being can direct the way.
- **Visualization can be a powerful tool.** After all, you can only be as perfect as your imagination will allow you to be.

Part IV

COACHING MATCHES

Chapter

11

PREPARING FOR MEETS AND MATCHES

You can do several things to prepare for competition. Knowing the tendencies, strengths, and weaknesses of your opponent can help. In this chapter, you'll see that I recommend scouting, videotape study, and statistical analysis as three ways to evaluate the upcoming opponent. Do your homework, but don't do it at the expense of performance in the main classroom, the mat, at practice and meets. Nobody will award you brownie points during a match for being able to critique the move that pinned you. Remember that the most important thing you can do to prepare for a match is to prepare your wrestlers. Avoid dwelling on the opponent or trying to influence things you have no control over. In the end it comes down to who's more skilled, better coached and drilled, and in superior condition.

PREPARING FOR THE FIRST MATCH

Wrestlers need to be especially careful when preparing for the first match of a tournament or a dual meet. Jumping out of bed and onto a wrestling mat doesn't work unless you're wrestling someone who has the same problem. For a 9:00 a.m. match, wrestlers should rise no later than 6:30 a.m. and should immediately have something to eat. A small but nutritionally balanced meal, with an emphasis on carbohydrates (such as cereal, toast, fruit, or juice), is perfect. After resting for 30 to 45 minutes, the wrestler should take a hot shower and receive a light massage.

Now the wrestler is ready for a thorough warm-up, pushing extra hard to blow out the cobwebs that accumulated overnight. When he feels ready, especially in the morning, he should spend a few extra minutes sprinting or wrestling hard and take the time to have another shower and rehydrate. The wrestler should keep ready by relaxing and stretching. About 8:50, or 10 minutes before match time, he should increase his pace so that by match time his heart rate is elevated again and ready to go maximum once the whistle blows. This type of warm-up helps prevent slow starts and hitting the wall early and can get wrestlers into the right intensity level for the whole match.

Proper warm-up and preparation increase a wrestler's chances of finishing strong at the end of the match and minimize his chances of injury. The chances of an upset in early morning matches can be greater because the discipline needed to win is more demanding. All too often individuals and teams bypass necessary match preparation. The later in the day the match begins, the easier it is to get in the best routine for match preparation.

PREPARING FOR MULTIPLE MATCHES

When facing multiple matches in the same day with very little time between them, pay special attention to nutrition and hydration. Stay aware of where your athletes are and what they do. It's a good idea to "camp" together as a team. Not only can you monitor your athletes better, you can also locate and share information with them more easily. Having food and drink located in the same area is a good idea as well. Anytime there is a significant break between matches, having your athletes go through a cool-down routine (jogging, stretching, keeping hydrated, snacking, showering, and having a massage) will be very beneficial. With very little time between matches, staying warm and hydrated will suffice.

PREPARING FOR NORMAL DUALS

This section details the preparation for a typical dual meet scheduled to start at 7:30 P.M. The timing of weigh-in will determine exactly

when you do certain steps in preparing for a match. If the weigh-in is at noon, here's how an athlete should prepare from the time he leaves weigh-in to the time of the match:

1. He takes in some fluids.
2. He gets a balanced pre-match meal with emphasis on carbohydrates (such as pasta, pancakes, baked potato, fruit, juice, or soup).
3. He rests and relaxes. If rest is not possible right after lunch due to school or another obligation, he gets one to two hours of rest sometime before the match.
4. Around 4:30 or 5:00, he eats a light snack and relaxes afterwards.
5. At 5:30, the wake-up begins. He walks, listens to music, showers, or does whatever helps make him more alert. Wrestlers should be aware of spending too much of their valuable and needed energy before they compete, however. For example, they shouldn't get too caught up in their teammates' competitions before their own. Now the wrestler is ready for the main warm-up, which is similar to the routine mentioned earlier for the 9:00 A.M. match, starting at the 7:30 A.M. time.

New Weight Rules

After the 1998 collegiate wrestling season, more emphasis and concern for weight-loss control and management was introduced. This is one area in the history of wrestling that needs to be changed. An excessive amount of water loss has been associated with wrestling and now needs to be disassociated. Studies have shown that performance is negatively affected by excessive water loss, as well as more important health concerns.

To eliminate the incentives of water weight reduction, rule changes for weighing in close to match time have been put in place. With one- or two-hour weigh-ins in place, athletes will have to focus on or be more aware of their actual weight during their match preparations. This annoyance can be less of a distraction, as long as one's weight is not a problem. The actual weight of the wrestler will determine the amount of the pre-match meal. Ideally, two and a half to three hours before match time, a carbohydrate-emphasized meal (snack) should be consumed.

Weigh-ins will occur at either two hours or one hour before the match. At one and a half to two hours before the match, a hot shower and stretching, along with a strong mental focus should be taking place. If already weighed in, wrestling warm-ups should begin at the one hour, 15 minute pre-match time. If weigh-in has not occurred yet, start as soon as logistically possible.

PREPARING FOR KEY COMPETITIONS

Key competitions and post-season tournaments allow breaks between rounds. Unlike the normal dual match routine, your athletes will be on different schedules. You need to make sure each individual has his nutritional needs met in a timely manner without having to wait for the entire team to eat. During a break, no competing athletes should go more than two hours without taking in food and fluids.

One of my goals is to develop an atmosphere and environment at Iowa that prepares wrestlers for the important events at the end of the season. To help the team's big match preparation, I schedule tough matches away from home during the season. Going into a hostile environment to battle a tough opponent tests your wrestlers' readiness and puts them in an environment that might be similar to what they'll face in conference, state, or national tournaments. I like to have the team compete in arenas that are like the ones the team will be in at the end of the season. This type of scheduling helps eliminate the fear factors that sometimes happen in big arenas

or events. It's invaluable experience for young wrestlers. Who knows, maybe not going to visit the nationals' site (University of North Carolina at Chapel Hill) in 1994 was a lack in preparation that cost Iowa the title!

LESSONS FROM POOR PREPARATION

Although you never want to see an athlete fail, sometimes the lessons learned from losing can encourage them to prepare more diligently for matches in the future. A wrestler who is unable to control his emotions, comes up short in conditioning, lacks confidence, and doesn't approach his matches with the discipline necessary is going to get a rude awakening at some point. It's just a matter of time before a tougher, better conditioned, more prepared wrestler takes it to him.

A coach can only do so much to convince some of the more stubborn-minded individuals that match preparation is an essential, everyday thing. What a coach can do is to try to make sure that when his poorly prepared athlete gets his lesson in preparation that it is a meaningful and positive one that will benefit the rest of his wrestling career. A crushing defeat is not the time for "I told you so." Instead, approach the situation unemotionally, pointing out to the athlete where the shortcomings in preparation exist and how he can correct them.

GOING INTO THE MATCH

Just as you expect your athletes to be prepared for competition, you've got to be prepared too. Part of this preparation is knowing the rules and how referees will make calls. No matter what level you coach, rules do change, and every coach and athlete should study the rules and know them well so they can use them to their advantage. Sometimes a rule change might favor a certain type of wrestler, but if he and his coach aren't aware of it, then that advantage is wasted. Every year the NCAA rules committee produces a rules video. This

Crash Course Leads to Title

Lincoln McIlravy, in his first year at Iowa, sat on the sidelines during November, December, and January until the first week of February. Four weeks before the Big Ten Championships began, I let Lincoln wrestle, thinking he could contribute to the team as well as win an NCAA title himself. His first meet was a home dual against Northwestern, and he was turned every which way but loose. Lincoln had looked great throughout practices and did exceptionally well in unattached competitions, but the mental part of wrestling in varsity competition seemed too much for Lincoln to overcome; things looked bleak.

One hope was to try something creative with Lincoln. To prepare him for a couple more big matches, the team set up a meet environment in the next practice. Fans were brought in, crowd noise was piped in, a referee officiated his matches, and the scoreboard was lit up. Lincoln wrestled on the main floor of Carver-Hawkeye Arena to add to the match-like experience.

I picked opponents for him that I thought would challenge him in a variety of ways, but that he could succeed against if he wrestled well. By the end of the week, instead of having only one match (against Northwestern) experience, Lincoln had what was almost the equivalent of a season of home dual matches under his belt. Lincoln showed progress throughout the week, winning all of the matches and dominating opponents by the end of the week.

Both of his varsity matches the next weekend were tough ones, and he pulled them out. He felt more comfortable and showed flashes of the dominating form I saw in practices. His confidence was building. Next was a road test at Iowa State, and boy did he come on there! He made a statement to the college wrestling ranks that he had arrived. By the time the NCAA tournament rolled around, he was ready for the best. Lincoln won an exciting 17-16 match to take the NCAA title as a true freshman with only a little more than a month of varsity experience.

Lincoln McIlravy needed fast learning experience, expertise, and adjustments to make him a veteran before winning the NCAA title as a freshman.

video is required viewing for college coaches. High school coaches should check with their state associations and the National Federation of State High School Associations to keep up with rule changes.

With regard to referees, it's naive to think that each referee will call a match the same way. Coaches don't coach in the same way, and wrestlers don't wrestle in the same way. The wise coach tries to read the referee before the match and then helps his wrestlers make any necessary adjustments in their approach. Understanding how a referee will make calls can directly affect the outcome of a match.

SCOUTING

The NCAA allows no expenses for nonrevenue-producing sports such as wrestling, but that isn't an excuse for failing to study and know your competition. These are the details that go along with being a prepared coach or wrestler. Check out and become familiar with the surroundings at home and away competition facilities. Keep in mind that home mat advantage definitely applies in wrestling.

In Carver-Hawkeye Arena, Iowa is 3-0 in NCAA tournaments. Iowa is 2-0 at home Big Ten championships with the point record being established during the 1983 event in Iowa City. Of the 10 weight classes in those Big Ten Championships, Iowa won nine of them. Iowa's dual meet record in Carver from 1983 through 1997 was 98-1, with the only loss a tight 19-18 match in 1988.

Video Study

Videotape is a big help in match preparation. It helps you and your wrestlers review their performances. Tape as many of your and your opponents' matches as possible. One caution here: when videotaping opposing teams and wrestlers, get approval before you do so. Exchanging videos with other coaches is also another way of helping prepare for your competitions. A video library should be a high priority for your program. If you have one, make sure it's accessible to the coaching staff and wrestlers, but also set up a system that makes everyone who has access to the tapes accountable. Accessibility and accountability are the key words for a video library.

Because wrestling doesn't have many televised matches, taping events on TV isn't an option for most coaches. Iowa Public Television has been offering some great matches for purchase. For more information, you can write: Iowa Public Television, 6450 Corporate Drive, P.O. Box 6450, Johnston, IA 50131, or call Doug Brooker at 800-532-1290. USA Wrestling also offers some essential videos for your program. These tapes show the best wrestlers; the World and Olympic Championships videos are the best ones to buy. Also, I've developed a video called *Competitor Supreme* that you can order by calling 1-800-HAWKSHOP.

Studying Statistics

In this age of technology and computers, you can put together an easy-to-use system for your athletes or your opponents with a simple push of a few buttons. In this system, you can store facts about your team, information about opponents' skills and techniques, and other important data. Statistics can aid your success. Knowing individual and team strengths and weaknesses can help your preparation. Used wisely, statistics can help a lesser wrestler upset a better wrestler by choosing the right strategy in the right place and the right time.

By studying statistics of your team or your opponents, you can learn what your practice time should emphasize. If statistics of your team's performance aren't consistent with your philosophy, you need to make changes. On a basic level, if your team is behind in takedowns and gives up riding time, your win-loss record is probably in jeopardy. Of course, if your team has the ideal statistic—all pins for your team, none against—then your takedowns and escapes don't matter as much.

War Stories

Sometimes you can improve readiness and motivation for a competition by sharing stories from previous experiences and matches during practices. Old war stories of past athletes and teams that have been successful can be described and acted out to catch your athletes' attention. New war stories emerge every year, especially with great teams and wrestlers. Lincoln McIlravy has several war stories that a coach could tell for years. One of the best comes from the NCAA finals match during his freshman year. It's a good one to tell to help relations between the coaches and athletes.

You Gotta Believe

Down by five points in the last 50 seconds of the NCAA title match, freshman Lincoln McIlravy begins to think that the end is near. Lincoln remembers it like this: "I'm ready to quit or at least start thinking defeat, but I look over to my coaches in the corner and they're still encouraging me to score. So I think, if they still believe I can win, why shouldn't I? After a couple of takedowns, a stalling call, and a takedown with two seconds remaining, I had come all the way back to win. My opponent had been ahead the entire match, except at the end, when it counted! I have to give my coaches the credit for believing in me even when I was doubting myself."

PRE-MATCH TALKS

Just as with any other communication with your athletes, your pre-meet talk will depend on the situation. What I say before an early-season, low-key tournament on the road may differ from what I say before a late-season, all-important dual match at home. Part of knowing what to say is keying in to your wrestlers' needs. Those needs can include going over individual strategy, discussing team goals, or hearing a short motivational speech. Some athletes may thrive on being fired up by the coach; others may prefer to prepare by themselves.

What you want to remember is that it's your job to help each athlete go in prepared, and that preparation may differ according to the time of year, the type of competition, and the makeup of your athletes. My final pre-meet talk happens shortly before the introduction of the athletes and includes small reminders of how to compete well. This kind of talk will help give your athletes an edge in competition. The other pre-meet talks happen early enough to have the real effect of helping the athlete get prepared for competition.

Making a Statement

Before the Big 10 and NCAA tournaments of 1997, several articles were being printed about what to expect at these events. Considering the fact that Iowa was not the tournament favorite, some of the articles were explaining why. One particular article talked about "too many holes in Iowa's lineup"; therefore, its chances were slim. On the day of individual talks to the team, my starting 177-pound wrestler, Tony Ersland, expressed dissatisfaction with being referred to as a hole in the Iowa lineup.

I'd been working on Tony's physical and mental toughness for quite some time, but it seemed to be at somewhat of a standstill. He was not predicted (by outsiders) to even get through the qualifiers, let alone score several points at the NCAA tournament. Well, he did just that, and I vividly remember his reaction—he was full of determination when he discussed his upcoming team contributions.

You never know what will trip an athlete's trigger. One approach I've found that works well is giving each wrestler a turn or two to talk to the team before big meets or tournaments. I'll do this usually toward the end of

Red Toenail Lesson

To make up the point deficit Iowa had going into the '97 NCAA Championships, the team had a two-point plan. One, score with majors and falls. Two, stay in the championship round for as long as possible. These two points were emphasized over and over again immediately after the Big 10 Championships through the NCAA Championships. In retrospect, these two points, especially the first one, elevated one young man's match tactics to a new level.

Jessie Whitmer, Iowa's small guy, had a tendency to coast to victory and often times let up somewhat before his matches ended, sometimes costing him the match. With the team championship at risk, Jessie was in a position late in his first two or three matches to score again and get Iowa extra team points. That's exactly what he did; in the process, he learned something very important about himself. He now consciously or subconsciously realized he could wrestle the whole match hard. The early team bonus point matches gave Jessie the determination and staying power to win quarter, semi, and final matches, each of which were not decided until the last 30 seconds.

Another factor in Jessie's success was a bit more unique, and demonstrates the power of one's beliefs. Before the first round of the NCAA Championships, I noticed something peculiar in the locker room. Jessie's toenails were painted red—something I hadn't noticed during the season. I asked Jessie, "What's going on?" He told me he needed something to fire him up. I said, "Red toenails?" Jessie said, "Coach, my girlfriend's toenails are painted red, and when I look at them, I get fired up. So I thought I'd paint mine to see if it would fire me up as well." By the quarterfinals, I was painting Jessie's toenails with red polish. Sometimes you have to do extra and unusual things (within reason) to bring about championship performances.

Under Jessie Whitmer's wrestling shoes are painted red toenails. You never know—something as small as this can make a difference in a wrestler's psyche.

the season in practice. The wrestler will tell his teammates and coaches his plan of action for winning Big Ten and NCAA titles. He'll talk about the attitude and effort he'll need to succeed. He usually doesn't guarantee victory, but these talks, which are often quite emotional, may pave the way for success. Used in this manner, a pre-meet talk can be as vital as the warm-up. It motivates the wrestler giving the speech and fires up the whole squad.

Every once in a while a coach should pull out a book of sayings and take the time to read and discuss them at the beginning of a practice or in a special classroom-type meeting. The right inspirational story or special way of expressing something important can have a positive impact on an athlete's mental preparation and toughness.

SUMMARY

Preparation for matches and meets involves many details and areas of concern. Experience is the best teacher in some cases, but other forms of preparation require work and study on your part. What worked one year or for one match may not be the best approach for the next year or even the next match. Try to establish a routine, but build in flexibility to meet the specific needs of the situation and personnel. Here are some key points to remember about preparation:

- Knowing your competition is important, but more important is focusing on your own preparation to maximize the abilities and performances of your athletes.
- Advance exposure of your athletes to competition sites is a worthwhile step in preparation; you'll see why when you add up your place points at the end of the season.
- Preparing your athletes for early morning matches, multiple matches, key matches, and end of the year tournament matches involves a lot of communication between the athletes and the coaches. Nutritional readiness is one area that demands close scrutiny, so be extremely knowledgeable here.
- Having athletes pay the price for their faults at specific times can help eliminate potential problem areas. Such problem areas might include a lack of control over emotions, weak conditioning, lack of confidence, and not knowing what to expect ahead of time.
- Pre-match and post-match talks and discussions can add to the motivation and success of your athletes. Sometimes these talks are more effective one-on-one; other times they're more effective in a team setting.
- Statistics, videos, and war stories can help you win if you know how to use them effectively.

Chapter 12

COACHING MATCHES

There's nothing like the heat of battle to get your blood flowing. I get more excited about coaching matches than I used to get when I competed. Anyone who's seen me on the sidelines urging my wrestlers on knows that I get pretty emotional and intense during a match. How I coach matches just naturally flows out of my personality. It would be inappropriate for coaches with more laid-back personalities to emulate my style; each coach needs to develop his own style and approach to coaching matches. Within your own approach, however, you should address basic principles and points in order to help your team succeed. I'll share some of those key points with you in this chapter.

WARMING UP

Try to warm up free from the crowd and other distractions. This is usually easier to do at home, where you can control the environment. My team warms up for meets in our practice area while our opponents warm up on the meet mat in front of our home crowd. This atmosphere allows me to communicate more easily with my athletes, who can focus on the task before them.

Of course, the team faces a more difficult situation on the road. It can be disconcerting to warm up in front of a crowd on the road, so you need to help your athletes concentrate on their mission. Even the rowdiest crowd will soon become silent once the match starts and your athletes are prepared, focused, and winning. Winning comes easier on the road when you know what to expect so you can make adjustments or prepare your team for the environment you'll be entering. For example, there's nothing worse than a band blaring in your ears when you're trying to concentrate, shout instructions, or encourage your athletes. You need a good set of lungs to outshout a whole horn section.

The nature of the competition will often dictate how you handle the match surroundings. You could go as far as keeping your wrestlers away from the match atmosphere until their competition time. Some athletes may have trouble conserving their energy and remaining focused if they appear too early before a large and festive crowd. Others can handle this distraction, but by and large, it's best in big meets to let your athletes prepare in private, where they can stoke their competitive fires and focus on their upcoming match.

READING THE REFEREE

Usually referees meet each team before a dual meet begins. Athletes and coaches should pay close attention to the referee's demeanor and words. If you don't get a good feel for how calls will be made before the match begins, you should get a good read a few minutes into the competition. Your athletes may need to adjust their attack according to how calls are going. It's up to you to help them understand how to adjust.

That said, I still believe that wrestlers need to make their own breaks in a match and not be consumed with how a referee is making calls. When a wrestler enters a match in excellent condition and with a proper attitude, the referee's calls usually won't be a factor. I stress this attitude with my wrestlers. Referees respect coaches and athletes who are prepared and who compete with intensity. Although it pays to get a good read on the referee, it pays even more to be prepared and to wrestle aggressively.

USING THE BEST STRATEGY

You always want your wrestlers to wrestle aggressively—that should be part of the strategy all wrestlers employ. Certainly it's ideal for a wrestler to be in an attacking position at all times. In the majority of cases, this position works to the wrestler's advantage.

A wrestler needs to know more than just how to attack, however. A wrestler needs to read the situation at hand, taking into account his own strengths and weaknesses as well as his opponent's. At times it's to a wrestler's advantage to work on wearing down his opponent's effectiveness. This is especially true early in the match if an opponent has proven his dominance before. But even in the latter case, where an opponent has dominated your wrestler in previous matches, there's a fine line between risking being too aggressive and limiting your own attack by being too defensive.

This is not a simple call on the coach's part, and I don't have any quick-and-easy guidelines for you to follow regarding strategy. I will say that there's great risk in changing your tactics at random. Even if an opponent dominated one of your wrestlers before, don't just arbitrarily change your approach. Making such a change on a whim, without thinking through the consequences, leaves the door wide open for your opponent to dominate again. Instead, plan an attack in a different way, but make it one that your wrestler has practiced and is prepared to use. Otherwise, the results can be dismal.

Strategic Mistakes

Tom Brands' Belo-Russian opponent in the 1994 World Championships in Istanbul was well known for always attacking to the left. So, naturally enough, Tom became bent on protecting his left side. The only problem was he became so obsessed with it that he forgot about his own attack, which is his bread and butter. Sure enough, Tom's opponent kept attacking to the left during the whole match. Tom, in defending the attacks, lost the match.

During those same championships, Melvin Douglas changed his stance for his Iranian opponent without even practicing it. In doing so, Melvin never did get his offense started, and he played right into his opponent's hands. Again, the last-minute change in tactics resulted in a loss. Both strategies were big mistakes, not because they were changes in tactics, but because they weren't practiced enough, and they didn't allow for an offensive attack to take place.

Change is fine when the athlete is prepared for it and when his offense isn't taken away from him. Not having a solid offensive plan in place is like sending a baseball batter to the plate without a bat. How's he supposed to get a hit when he doesn't have anything to hit with? Although you should stay away from big

changes, making a minor adjustment or a small tactic change is sometimes the right thing to do.

ON THE SIDELINES

For big matches, it's best to have an assistant keep track of the time and score and inform you of any mistakes being made. One extra second of riding time, one extra second on the clock, and errors in scoring have made the difference in some important matches. Although referees' calls can be difficult to handle, it's much more difficult to lose a match because of a scorekeeper's or timekeeper's error. Having an assistant keep on top of these

Winning Desire

Talk about attitude, four-time Big Ten champion Mike DeAnna (Iowa wrestler from 1977 to 1981) overcame skin cancer during his career at Iowa with a surgery that removed skin, tissue, and muscle that was cancer-prevalent. After his surgery, Mike took a red-shirt year and came back with the same performance and attitude that it takes to be the best.

Battling back is often part of the game. Mike DeAnna fought cancer and came back in his final year to his fourth Big Ten title, as well as becoming an All-American again.

matters will free you up to pay full attention to your wrestlers.

On the sidelines, I focus on how my wrestlers are performing both physically and mentally. I look for them to be executing holds effectively and to be aggressively attacking, and I'm strongly urging them to put themselves in the best position to win. I tell my wrestlers to stay in their best positions and to execute their best holds. Although I'll often encourage experimenting with new holds in practice, I discourage it during matches. Why bank on something you haven't practiced or mastered? I also emphasize to my wrestlers to never concede position. Doing so allows opponents to get in offensive position. When two evenly matched wrestlers face each other, the one who concedes position first inevitably ends up losing.

Usually a wrestler's desire flags and he begins to concede position when one of four things happens:

- He becomes tired.
- He becomes lazy.
- He loses concentration.
- He doesn't have as aggressive an attitude as his opponent.

The latter three are more likely when number one (fatigue) happens. All four have to do with physical and mental toughness and conditioning. Desire plays such an important factor in winning and losing, not only in athletic contests, but in many facets of life.

PERSONAL CONDUCT

Wrestling is an intense sport. We coaches drum it into our athletes to be aggressive, to attack, to be intense, to not concede position. In the next breath, we tell them to be perfect gentlemen, to conduct themselves with class and dignity, to respect their opponents and referees, and to be nice and polite in public. This may sound like a conflicting message, but it's not. Both goals can be accomplished. You can compete with fiery intensity and still carry yourself with class. Coaches can and should be role models of that behavior. That said, it's still

not easy for athletes to rein in their emotions when their match is finished; some athletes will need more help than others in this area.

10 Seconds and Counting

Terry Brands is a fiery competitor. He also can have a hard time controlling his emotions, especially on a rare loss. He's not someone who can just turn his emotions on and off, so I helped him develop a ritual to help him control his temper and avert potential problems. The ritual is an old one. He simply steps back from the middle of the mat and counts to 10 before stepping forward to shake his opponent's hand.

Some people have seen this ritual as unsportsmanlike, but they don't understand Terry. He needs the time to calm down after an emotional loss which, thank God, does not happen often. Sometimes little rituals can save a disastrous scene. I think it's much better to help a person adjust rather than expect him to fit someone else's idea of a perfect mold.

AFTER THE MATCH

Although it's best not to have your team just run off after a match, it's also probably best to save any in-depth evaluation for later. You'll be in a better position to evaluate once you've reviewed the match tapes and slept on your ideas. It's too easy to overreact in the heat of the moment and give what you later realize is not the most helpful evaluation. In some cases, you'll feel the need to say something to your wrestlers, but weigh that decision against the benefit of saying it the next day, after you've thought it through.

Deciding when to evaluate a match can be a tough call. Taking into account what is happening with your team and what part of the season it is might help you choose when to address the team. Sometimes things cannot wait, or it will be too late. The philosophy of what goes on in the wrestling room stays in the wrestling room is an unwritten rule. Once something is said or done, however, it has the potential to later be misperceived by others. Hopefully, any misunderstandings can be easily straightened out due to your good rapport with your athletes.

Many times when an athlete hasn't performed well he knows why. If he's gotten off-track in trying to attain his goals, then he has to decide whether he wants to make the extra effort it will take to get there. That kind of effort is evidenced by athletes who work on their conditioning immediately following their matches. This conditioning work may involve hard sprints, more wrestling, or intense exercising. It doesn't have to take long, maybe 10 minutes. When athletes are dedicated enough to work out after a match, you know they're willing to pay the price to achieve their goals.

Working Out Frustration

Tom Brands' goal of winning four Big Ten titles was shattered in his junior year by Dave Zuniga of Minnesota. Immediately after the match I found Tom out in a big field next to the Northwestern gym doing 100-yard sprints. It helped cool him down tem-

per-wise. Even as he was sprinting, he was starting to focus on the NCAA Championships in two weeks. At those Championships, he won the title by defeating Zuniga in a barn-burning match.

SUMMARY

Be as prepared to coach as your wrestlers are to wrestle. That includes knowing how to use your school's environment to your advantage and knowing how to handle difficult road environments. It also includes knowing the rules and getting a good read on how the referee will make calls.

Help your athletes focus on their best strategy for their matches, encouraging them to stay in their best positions and to execute their best holds. Any change in major tactics should be considered and practiced long before a meet. Teach your athletes to wrestle with fierce intensity but control their emotions after a match. Speaking of post-match time, it's usually better to save any type of in-depth evaluation for later after you've had time to view tapes, wind down, and think more clearly.

Part V

COACHING EVALUATION

Chapter

13

EVALUATING WRESTLERS' PERFORMANCES

Coaches are continually evaluating wrestlers' performances at practice, at early-season tournaments, and on into season-ending championships. Evaluation never stops, on either a team or an individual basis. There is a big difference, of course, between simply observing performances and evaluating them. Any knowledgeable coach can observe performances and see what's working and what isn't; the coach who uses that information to help his wrestlers improve is the one who will elevate his program.

Immediate success is always wanted but rarely achieved. More common is gradual improvement and eventual success resulting from ongoing evaluation, feedback, and development of every wrestler. Through evaluations and adjustments, programs on the bottom can work their way to the top.

YOUR SQUAD

You'll begin the evaluation process in pre-season by choosing your squad. Hopefully mat space is not a problem and you can keep all of the wrestlers who wish to participate and are willing to work. In terms of quantity, my philosophy has always been the more the merrier. Ideally, I like to have two competitive athletes at each weight, plus another one for every other weight. I also like to have at least 10 walk-ons. However, realistically the team usually ends up with 30 to 35 athletes. It doesn't attract the number of walk-ons that I'd like because of the level of the program. With fewer than 10 scholarships, it's hard to bring in 25 competitive wrestlers.

Having an abundance of wrestlers is a nice headache to have. At some high schools, simply filling a roster can be a problem. High school coaches have to be great recruiters to make sure they have adequate numbers for all the weight classes—especially when they're trying to fill rosters for freshman, junior varsity, and varsity teams. Any coach would much prefer filling those spots with young men who come out for the sport of their own volition to succeed in wrestling, but the reality is that many coaches will have to actively seek out the athletes who can competently fill their open spots. The athletes are out there, but you may have to go out and find them.

That's where a good feeder system is crucial to building your program. Get to know the coaches and the young wrestlers who are involved in programs in middle schools, junior highs, and in local clubs. These connections may prove invaluable to you as you attempt to build your roster. As you're seeking athletes, you don't want to paint too drastic a picture, or they won't want to go out for the team. At the same time, you don't want any athletes quitting, so you should spell out what they're getting into. Forfeits don't help promote the sport.

I want my wrestlers to finish what they start. That applies not only to sticking with the team, but to finishing holds, gutting through workouts, and reaching their goals. If an athlete says he's going to climb the rope five times, he should climb it five times. Sell the athletes on the benefits of wrestling and of participating in your program, let them know what your basic expectations are in terms of attendance and effort, and encourage them to go out for the team. Once you have your final squad, you'll evaluate how they size up in the weight classifications.

Filling the Weight Classes

I'm a firm believer in filling all the weight classes with competitive wrestlers. I prefer to build athletes up physically rather than slowing their body growth process, however. Putting the onus on the wrestler to stay in a weight class that's too small for him isn't fair or healthy for young athletes. The onus should be on the coach to find a competitive wrestler who naturally fits into that weight category.

As you're considering in the pre-season how your wrestlers fit into the various weight classes, keep in mind that you may have to adjust your lineup throughout the year. First, wrestlers, especially in high school, may be growing and maturing and thus moving up in weight class. Second, you may be faced with one of those last-minute surprises: a high school senior decides to funnel his energy in a different direction as he prepares for his future. A family moves right before the season starts. A wrestler suffers an injury that's going to take some healing and rehabilitation time.

It pays to evaluate your roster and weight classifications throughout the year in part to minimize the effect of such surprises. The following sample charts will help you evaluate your roster. These types of charts help you focus on your recruiting needs as you see your roster holes. It also helps you evaluate your roster in important areas such as effectiveness, attitude, likelihood of staying in school, possibility of growing, scholarship money available, and so on.

As mentioned, growth spurts can make the high school, and sometimes college, years unpredictable. Looking at each athlete's family traits and history as well as considering his body type can help you predict what weight class he is progressing toward. I include space for years before and beyond the high school years because both are important in the wrestler's career. The years before high school help determine the number and quality of athletes on your team; the years beyond affect not only the wrestler's future in college competition and beyond, but the promotion of the sport as well.

EVALUATING PRACTICE PERFORMANCES

You should be continually evaluating your wrestlers in practice: Is their stamina where it should be? Do they need to develop more

Middle School and High School Recruiting Chart

	7th	8th	9th	10th	11th	12th	College-bound wrestlers
103							
112							
119							
125							
130							
135							
140							
145							
152							
160							
171							
189							
HWT							

College Roster

	Recruits (h.s. senior or junior college)	Red Shirts	Frosh	Soph	Juniors	Seniors	Olympians
125							
133							
141							
149							
157							
165							
174							
184							
197							
285							

strength? Are they executing moves and holds well? Are they aggressive, are they strong in their attack, are they playing to their strengths? Do they have the proper attitude? Are minor injuries cropping up? Do they have their body weight under control?

Only by continually reading your athletes can you tell when to help them make adjustments. If, for example, your wrestlers begin to suffer minor injuries, you need to consider what's causing those injuries and adjust accordingly. It may be that they're tiring late in practice and need more conditioning, or perhaps they need more strength. Regardless, it's imperative that you make adjustments if you don't want a roster full of injured wrestlers. Sometimes adjustments involve the whole team, and sometimes they pertain only to an individual. Simply changing practice opponents can sometimes help get a wrestler back on track.

To know when to make these adjustments, you'll need to not only understand your wrestlers, but also the sport of wrestling. Helping your athletes get to the next level takes great knowledge on the coach's part, not only in helping an athlete choose the next move, but in knowing when to step in and help an athlete adjust and when to let that athlete work through a challenging period in his development as a wrestler. Although I'd love to say that this decision gets easier as the season progresses, it often becomes more difficult. One thing that can help you make that decision easier is a video camera.

Videotaping athletes during workouts can be helpful in a couple of ways. First, you can review the tape on your own and then later with individual wrestlers, going over the holds they need to improve. Second, the tapes don't lie. It's amazing what they can reveal about a wrestler's work ethic. I've seen some wrestlers, the great ones, leave practice with a thousand executions to their credit. Other wrestlers leave with no executions and then they wonder why they're not winning their matches. The wrestlers who are getting little accomplished in practice are usually surprised by what the camera catches: a lot of standing around, taking breathers, and so on.

Seeing themselves on tape, whether to study their holds or to understand how they can get more out of themselves in practice, can be both instructional and motivating to wrestlers. Try not to let the wrestlers know you're taping, because that might affect their approach to practice. Those who are "dogging it" will get the message to turn the effort up when they see themselves on tape. Hopefully, though, your wrestlers won't need a videotape to motivate them to take their wrestling to another level as the season progresses. That motivation should come from within as they prepare for big matches or tournaments.

TURNING IT UP A NOTCH

Reading your wrestlers as they approach a tough competition or a late-season tournament is not always easy. They are beginning to peak both physically and mentally, and tempers can flare as they prepare for those big competitions. When you help your wrestlers prepare for big meets, tension can mount, because it takes renewed and higher commitments to achieve new levels. It may be easier for you to back off, but doing so won't help your wrestlers reach their potential. As you are probably well aware, wrestlers can get just plain ornery, especially toward the end of the season, and things can get pretty ugly in the practice room.

The Penalty Box

When things get especially ugly, Iowa has a penalty box where athletes are sent to cool off. I have an even tighter control at my disposal that I call my zero level of tolerance. When a wrestler passes my zero level of tolerance, usually by making excuses for something that was quite avoidable, he's out of the practice room. My zero level of tolerance is tested most often by a talented individual whose work ethic is poor. I usually give warnings, but when an athlete continues the behavior after a final warning or commits an inexcusable act, it's either to the penalty box or to the showers.

Turning It Up by Tuning It Down

Iowa won the 1997 Big Ten Championships, but did not perform at the level needed to win the NCAA Championship. I knew I needed to pull something out of my hat for a much better performance in two weeks. I needed to peak the team better, to present a challenge that would create an edge. Instead of single practices every day, I switched the team to two shorter practices daily. By the end of the first day, the athletes were taxed both physically and mentally. I was heading in the wrong direction. They did not complain because they knew I was doing what I felt was needed to be successful in the NCAA Championships, and I had a pretty good track record.

The team was supposed to do the two-a-days for three days straight. The second day I canceled practice except for the sauna and massage. After that, I eased up on the physical preparation for the national tournament and focused on the mental side. The rest rejuvenated the team, and their mental outlook improved accordingly. The team went into the tournament primed and performed exceptionally well, winning the national title and breaking the scoring record. In fact, several records were accomplished by tuning it down in physical preperation.

EVALUATING MATCH PERFORMANCES

Although evaluating your athletes' performances in practice is an essential component in evaluating their progress, nothing tells a truer tale than seeing them perform in matches. On every team, there are probably some athletes who perform better in practice and some who seem to save it for matches. It often takes several matches before you can get a true read on how a wrestler is performing. One lesson I've learned is to not give up on wrestlers who seem to fall flat in practice.

BRINGING OUT ATHLETES' POTENTIAL

On the other extreme are the athletes who look like superstars in practice but who don't perform up to their potential in matches. Most often this problem is more psychological than physical, and it can be extremely frustrating for coaches as well as athletes. Such a problem is probably more prevalent at the high school level, but it can happen as well at the college level, particularly with walk-on athletes. Sometimes it can happen to a wrestler who has been successful in the past but who has recently suffered some difficult defeats. It's not easy to say why some athletes bounce back from these defeats more determined than ever while others see their match performances drop.

Whatever the circumstances, you need to analyze what might be holding your wrestler back and help him over this psychological hump. It's not an easy task, especially at the collegiate level, where you might be working with an athlete who has years of a psychologically debilitating pattern already ingrained. Each athlete has a different set of experiences and a certain button to push in terms of motivation and match performance. One unusual case was the wrestler who responded best to his father's blunt criticism. I asked the kid if he wanted to avoid his dad's harsh comments, but he said it helped him push himself to improve and that treatment was okay. Although unusual, this approach worked well for him.

You can approach these problems in several ways. To help athletes reach their full potential in matches, I have done the following:

- Simulated life-like matches in practice.

- Entered wrestlers in outside competitions where they were more likely to experience success.

- Set up visits with sports psychologists and communicated with close family to determine if they had any facts, ideas, or suggestions to help bring the best out in matches.

- Created a pre-match environment that was most conducive to a wrestler going in mentally prepared.

A Diamond in the Rough

Randy Lewis, one of Iowa's greatest all-time performers, couldn't score a point in his first two months of practice as a freshman. In the tryout for his weight class, he went against a teammate who had thoroughly dominated him in practice. To my great surprise, Randy won the tryout—the first evidence of greater things to come. At first I thought maybe Randy just got lucky, especially when the team returned to normal practices and he continued to be dominated. Randy was the one who dominated in his matches, however. He was a "gamer"; he completely changed his mental approach when he performed in matches.

Randy has not been my only gamer who really turned it on for matches. Others who also surprised me in their ability to pick it up for matches were Chris Campbell, Ed and Lou Banach, and Tom and Terry Brands. All of these athletes learned to wrestle better in practice, but it was a pleasure watching their matches because I knew I'd see a considerable gain in tempo.

Practice matches don't always tell the tale and Randy Lewis, two-time Iowa NCAA champion and 1984 Olympic gold medallist, is one of several wrestlers that turned it up for matches—where it really counts!

In the last case, some wrestlers might be helped by being away from the crowd and watching television, reading, or listening to music. Several wrestlers have liked me to slap them fairly hard on the jaw just before going out to wrestle. Of course, you want to make sure anyone witnessing this understands why you're doing it and that it's at the wrestler's request! Even then, I would recommend talking with the parents first to make sure this is okay with them.

One of your top priorities should be to help your athletes fully use their God-given abilities. Sometimes that means working hard to arrive at the method that will work best for them. Each set of circumstances is different, and each wrestler may need to be handled differently. Sometimes you can pick up on an athlete's slump by keeping records of their progress during the season. In doing so, you can see the peaks and valleys and perhaps know what precipitates the valleys and when to expect them.

CHARTING PROGRESS DURING THE SEASON

Keeping records of your athletes' practices can help explain their highs and lows, as mentioned. It can also show their progress and work ethic. You can keep records in practice notebooks, which are commercially available, or you can chart their progress in a

Gabes-

I was planning on giving this to you as a retirement gift, but considering your physical condition I think it is close enough. I saw this picture and thought of you instantly. You always mention in your lectures to my classes that you were like a horse with blinders. It is Secretariat winning the Triple Crown in the 1973 Belmont Stakes. This race has been considered by many to be *the most dominating performance in all of sports.* Those who believe that must not have been wrestling fans. I hope 1997 brings you good health. A wise man once told me, "If you don't have your health, work hard to get it."

If you look 31 lengths behind Secretariat, you can see Oklahoma State, Iowa State, Penn State, and a few other contenders. Had Secretariat been wearing the #1 on his silks, I think this would be a perfect analogy. If you truly were always a horse with blinders, however, you would have never gotten to know me. Best of luck to you this season and always.

Mitchell Kelly

spiral notebook. I use such charts not only to track my wrestlers' progress, but to motivate them as well.

For example, one year I stuck a gold star by each date when an athlete showed up on time and worked hard the whole practice. This star not only motivated many of the wrestlers to be on time and to finish hard, but it also pointed out the ones who were just sliding by. The people who were doing the bare minimum and not always getting the gold stars were usually the ones who were struggling most, both athletically and academically.

CHARTING OFF-SEASON WORKOUTS

Off-season workout charts also chart progress and track work ethic. The only difference here is that I post the charts in a central location, such as in the locker room or on my office door, and each athlete fills out his own chart. It's amazing how much these charts reveal about desire, work ethic, and progress as a wrestler and how success in the off-season workouts often spills over into success the next season and into success beyond the athletic arena.

Reviewing these charts lets you know who you can count on during the next season. It's not always the most successful wrestler, in terms of records, who is at the top of the off-season workout charts. It's very gratifying to see young wrestlers who maybe aren't as talented as others put so much effort into their off-season workouts. These athletes may not get the headlines during their wrestling careers, but you know they'll excel in their lives and the professions they choose.

Three of my former student-athletes immediately come to mind: Mitch Kelly, Mark Mysnyk, and Chris Gapen. Although they didn't turn out to be superstars on the mat, because

of their attitudes they have become doctors in academic and medical fields.

A NOTE ABOUT RECORDS

Records—and here I'm talking about things such as "three-time conference champion" or "two-time state (or NCAA) champion"—are like statistics: they can help you see strengths and weaknesses, but there's a danger in focusing too heavily on them. Don't let your wrestlers get caught up in trying to attain records. Wrestlers who focus on records bring on extra stress and pressure and end up hurting their performances. Instead, wrestlers should focus on executing properly and being prepared. If they do, the records and awards will come. Tell your wrestlers, "Do your homework religiously and in the end your records will be outstanding."

SUMMARY

Evaluation must be ongoing in any wrestling program. The issue is not when to evaluate, but how today's evaluation can help your wrestlers improve tomorrow. Videotaping your athletes in practice, using roster and workout charts, and using individual approaches to help athletes reach their potential are all part of the evaluation process. It takes a seasoned coach to know when to help an athlete make adjustments and when to let that athlete work through his current challenges without adjustment.

The bottom line in evaluating your wrestlers' progress is through actual competitions. Some wrestlers may not show what they're made of until they take to the mat against an opponent from another team. A large part of coaching is helping athletes reach their full potential—and that requires constant evaluation.

Chapter

14

EVALUATING YOUR PROGRAM

Post-season program evaluations can be just as valuable as in-season evaluations of your wrestlers. Program evaluations aren't just useful for programs where obvious improvements are needed or desired, even the most successful programs benefit from this process. I learned this the hard way in the mid-1980s, when, with a string of nine NCAA titles under my belt, I said, "If it's not broken, why fix it?" The answer became evident when that string of championships was broken. Through this experience, I learned the value of evaluating and making whatever changes are necessary to continue to improve.

That's what the evaluation process is about: improving. I evaluate my staff, my wrestlers, the equipment and facilities, and even the "product"—that is, the match environment and entertainment value. My staff and I usually go through this evaluation process shortly after the season ends. Although I prepare notes and open a general program evaluation meeting with my own remarks, I find it very helpful to hear what each member of my staff thinks. Hearing their thoughts and concerns has often resulted in uncovering issues and stopping little problems from becoming big.

EVALUATING YOUR STAFF

In addition to including your staff in a general program evaluation, you should evaluate your staff in order to keep your program running strong. No top program can operate without great assistants. There are so many facets to a program; a head coach can't hope to keep everything running smoothly without help from a multitalented staff. It's your job to assess your assistant coaches' strengths and to put them in positions where they can do what they do best. In a way, it's just like assessing your squad and filling out your weight classes position by position: in this case, you're assessing the needs of your program and making sure each facet is covered by the assistant most capable of handling the duty.

I'm fortunate to have had outstanding assistants. In the 1997 season, the coaching staff at Iowa included assistant coaches Jim Zalesky and Tom Brands and Terry Brands as a volunteer coach. All three of these coaches, along with Royce Alger, the strength and conditioning coach, were able to work with individual wrestlers in conditioning, strength training, and technique. Royce was also cleared to practice due to rules regarding Olympic contenders. They covered the whole room in practice, from lightweights through heavyweights. Each one also worked with certain wrestlers, which is an important point. Certain athletes hit it off better with certain coaches and seem to learn and advance more readily when paired off with these coaches. Keep this in mind as you provide your wrestlers one-on-one attention.

Speaking of attention, make sure you give your staff the recognition they deserve. Coaches who put in long hours for low pay need something to keep them going. Giving them credit through the media is one way to give them this recognition. Such recognition also helps your assistants build a name for themselves in the coaching community and makes them more marketable, should they decide to leave. Of course, acting to get their pay increased is another way of helping your staff.

Your goal should be to give your assistants the experience to move up into head coaching opportunities, if they so desire. Many assistants here at Iowa have moved into head coaching positions elsewhere after contributing to the program. I think it's a healthy situation for assistants to want to move up a level, and any evaluation of them should be with that in mind, as well as how they can help your program now.

EVALUATING YOUR WRESTLERS

Assistant coaches aren't the only ones who should want to move up a level. An individual champion one year must be a better wrestler the following year to remain a champion. Staying at the same level will not get the job done. If your wrestlers don't keep improving, they'll be passed by. It's that simple.

Second Place for Poor Evaluation

In the 1993–94 season, Iowa won the Big Ten conference title and placed second at the NCAA Championships. You'd think a coach would be pleased with these results, but I wasn't—at least not with the NCAA finish. In evaluating my team following the NCAA Championships, I concluded that it did not compete up to its ability at several weights.

If the team had finished second or anywhere else while performing up to its abilities, then I'd have had fewer reasons to be upset. Unfortunately, that wasn't the case. For some reason, my wrestlers held back on several occasions. To be physically beaten is one thing, to lose because of a lack of mental ability to win is inexcusable. I blame myself for not mentally preparing my athletes to win. Second place in this case rated a poor evaluation because of the team's inability to compete up to its potential.

When evaluating your athletes, ask yourself these questions:

- Did the team reach its potential?
- Did each athlete reach his potential? If not, what held him back?
- How could I have gotten more out of the wrestlers? Could someone else have gotten more out of them? If so, how?

If you feel your athletes have gotten all they could out of their talent, then you've been successful. That doesn't necessarily mean you as a team, or they as individuals, were the actual champions. Although if you have the talent and your team reached its potential, then championships are more likely. It's important to understand that team and individual records are affected by outside factors you can't totally control, but you can control whether you were able to help your wrestlers achieve their potential.

Wrestlers are also prime coaching candidates. As you can see from the list on page 196, many wrestlers I've coached are now coaches themselves.

EVALUATING EQUIPMENT AND FACILITIES

Part of the post-season evaluation includes assessing your equipment and facilities to make sure that they're safe and still usable. Now is the time to replace or update equipment and to make recommendations for needed facility changes. Certainly as you evaluate equipment and facilities, your priorities should be in maintaining safety and in keeping the necessary equipment in adequate shape and supply. If your budget allows for it, try to provide variety in your equipment, whether it's through new uniforms or through new workout equipment. This variety can spark your wrestlers' motivation and interest.

EVALUATING YOUR "PRODUCT"

You also want to motivate and interest another group: your fans. After the season's over, analyze how entertaining and exciting your matches were for the fans. One of your goals should be to make your matches exciting and appealing to attend. Don't be afraid to try different ideas. Remember, not all fans are there solely for the wrestling; they, just like any other audience, like to be entertained. In thinking of ways to add interest to your matches, you may end up attracting not just one person from a family, but the whole family. These ideas can be pretty subtle; the main goal is to broaden your appeal.

For instance, in addition to providing entertaining wrestling, Iowa looks for other touches: the P.A. announcer uses nicknames in introducing some of the wrestlers, and the pep band plays a bit of music from a song that each wrestler likes just as he steps onto the mat. These small gestures help fans identify with each wrestler. Fans themselves can organize some entertaining routines that can be fun and exciting. Before most meets and tourneys a great fan, Kirk Reeder, dressed in a black and gold tux and led the crowd in cheers to help get everyone hyped. Any positive reason to get fans more involved will help bring in more numbers. These extras are not earth shattering, but they add flavor to the environment. Another touch Iowa has is a meet program with highlights about each team. Probably one of the most important aspects of the program are the post-match socials where many fans gather and the coach mingles and speaks.

SUMMARY

Post-season evaluations are vital to the success of your program. The programs that stand pat are the ones that will be passed by. You need to assess how you can improve your program in all its facets. Assistant coaches can provide valuable feedback in evaluating the program, and they also deserve a thorough evaluation by you. Assess their strengths and put them in positions where they can use those strengths.

Each wrestler also deserves an evaluation regarding how close he came to his potential. The wrestlers' success in this area is directly tied to your success in helping them fully use their talents. Other areas that deserve assessment are equipment, facilities, and your overall product. You need to always be thinking of ways to make your product, the matches, interesting and appealing to a wide variety of fans. Once people come to your matches, they may become fans and supporters if you have a quality program. But you must work at getting them to the matches in the first place.

GABLE-COACHED WRESTLERS NOW COACHING

Aaron Aure	University of Northern Colorado
Terry Brands	University of Iowa
Tom Brands	University of Iowa
C.T. Campbell	Wilton High School (IA)
Mike Carpenter	Avon High School (OH)
Bart Chelesvig	University of Wisconsin
Tim Cysewski	Northwestern University
Barry Davis	University of Wisconsin
Morgan DePrenger	West Liberty High School (IA)
Kevin Dresser	Christiansburg High School (VA)
Eric Ehlen	Mt. Ayr High School (IA)
Tony Ersland	Central Michigan University
Travis Fiser	Grundy High School (VA)
Al Frost	Nashua-Plainfield High School (IA)
Duane Goldman	Indiana University
Andy Haman	Doherty High School (CO)
Dean Happel	Lisbon High School (IA)
Mike Hatcher	Durant High School (IA)
Jim Heffernan	University of Illinois
John Heffernan	St. Edwards High School (OH)
Curt Heideman	Cornell College
Mike Hruska	Schaumburg High School (IL)
Alan Hull	Raytown South High School (KS)
Dennis Hynek	Cedar Rapids Kennedy High School (IA)
Pat Kelly	Waldorf College
Dan Levy	Hersey High School (IL)
Steve Martin	Great Bridge High School (VA)
Mike McGivern	Des Moines Lincoln High School (IA)
Lincoln McIlravy	University of Iowa
Keith Mourlam	Virginia Tech University
Matt Nerem	Tipton High School (IA)
John Oostendorp	Coe College
Brad Penrith	University of Northern Iowa
Eric Pierson	Oak Grove High School (MO)
Greg Randall	Boise State University
David Ray	Northern Montana University
Mark Reiland	Solon High School (IA)
Tom Ryan	Hofstra University
Joel Sharratt	Minnesota State Developmental Coach
Charlie Sherertz	Whitfield High School (MO)
Brad Smith	Iowa City High School (IA)
Terry Steiner	University of Wisconsin
Troy Steiner	University of Wisconsin
Doug Streicher	Linn-Mar High School (IA)
Jessie Whitmer	Eagle Grove High School (IA)
Jim Zalesky	University of Iowa
Lennie Zalesky	Indiana University

Appendix

WRESTLING PUBLICATIONS

The following national wrestling publications should be subscribed to and read.

Amateur Wrestling News
P.O. Box 54679
Oklahoma City, OK 73154
405-843-9992
Contact: Ron Good

This publication covers college wrestling as well as some high school wrestling.

USA Wrestler
6155 Lehman Drive
Colorado Springs, CO 80918
719-597-8333
Contact: Gary Abbott

This publication includes all levels with an emphasis on international wrestling.

W.I.N.
P.O. Box 194
Newton, IA 50208
888-305-0606
Contact: Mike Chapman

This publication is for college coaches, fans, and anyone interested in other related disciplines. It also covers some high school wrestling.

Wrestling USA
109 Apple House Lane
Missoula, MT 59802
800-359-1850

This publication is written for high schoolers from a national point of view. It is also good for college coaches.

Several states have publications that cover their own states fairly well with an emphasis on high school wrestling. A list of those follow.

The American Grappler
P.O. Box 5205
Bloomington, IN 47407
812-334-4210

California Wrestler
220 Alder
Pacific Grove, CA 93950
408-649-5237

Center Mat
P.O. Box 7
Dawson, PA 15428
708-665-5406

Crossface Illinois/Wisconsin
4349 Pheasant Run
Janesville, WI 53546
608-758-8758

EIWA Newsletter
189 Spring Beauty Drive
Lawrenceville, NJ 08648
609-896-3476

Florida Amateur Wrestling News
110 Devon Drive
Clearwater, FL 34630
813-447-7662

Gilman Wrestling News
Box 423
Parkston, SD 57366

The Guillotine
Box 14
Glencoe, MN 55336
320-864-6880

The Head Lock
15113 Willow Creek Drive
Omaha, NE 68138
402-894-5502

The Inside Trip
1801 E. Fir Street
Cottonwood, AZ 86326
520-634-7531

The Louisiana Grappler
P.O. Box 55452
Metairie, LA 70055
504-845-8421

Maryland Wrestler
10086 Fair Beauty
Columbia, MD 21046
410-997-0575

Michigan Format
930 Forest Drive
Portage, MI 49002
616-378-2692

Michigan Wrestling News
P.O. Box 644
Clarkston, MI 48347
810-625-9501

Missouri Amateur Grappler
P.O. Box 28828
St. Louis, MO 63123
314-894-7422

North Carolina Mat News
414 Knollwood Drive
Kannapolis, NC 28083
704-933-8280

New Jersey Wrestler
P.O. Box 224
Liberty Corner, NJ 07938
908-766-5295

Ohio Wrestling Magazine
P.O. Box 582
Aurora, OH 44202
330-562-8371

On the Mat
2855 Roundtop Drive
Colorado Springs, CO 80918
303-791-4598

Oregon Wrestling Record
55 Kerr Parkway, #18
Lake Oswego, OR 97035

Pennsylvania Roundup
P.O. Box 774
Lock Haven, PA 17745
717-748-8887

The Predicament
P.O. Box 545
Emmetsburg, IA 50536
712-852-2288

The Summer Wrestling Guide
P.O. Box 131
Tabor, New Jersey 07878

Texas Mat Talk
8737 Grenadier Drive
Dallas, TX 75238
214-348-8548

Virginia Wrestling News
Mike Newbern, Editor
1000 Samuel Miller Loop
Charlottesville, VA 22903
804-572-4977

*Wrestling Review of Western
New York*
1285 Main Street
Buffalo, NY 14209
716-885-9016

Wrestling Tournament Update
2818 Salisbury Avenue
Edgemere, MD 21219
410-477-0748

ZIA Wrestling
P.O. Box 304
Arroyo Hondo, NM 87513

INDEX

Note: Page numbers in *italic* indicate illustrations; those in **boldface** indicate tables or forms.

ABOUT THE AUTHOR

THE GABLE COACHING RECORD

15 NCAA team titles
152 All-Americans
2536.75 NCAA points
45 National champions
78 NCAA finalists

Dan Gable is the most successful figure to ever wrestle and coach the sport. His accomplishments as an athlete on the mat and as a mentor for many years after that have established him as one of the greatest champions in all of sports.

As a high school wrestler in Waterloo, Iowa, Gable won all 64 of his matches and three state championships. At Iowa State University he compiled a 118-1 wrestling record, while claiming two NCAA championships. He still holds NCAA records with 24 straight pins and 99 straight victories.

At the 1972 Olympics, he won a gold medal without surrendering a single point to any of his six opponents. In his six Olympic matches and the 15 matches he went through to qualify for the Olympic team, Gable posted a 21-0 record and outscored his opponents 130-1. Gable's coaching record is even more impressive. During 21 seasons as head coach, his

University of Iowa teams won 15 NCAA championships and 21 Big Ten Conference championships. His teams had an unprecedented .932 winning percentage (355-21-5). He also coached the 1984 United States Olympic wrestling team to seven gold medals.

Gable has been inducted into both the Olympic Hall of Fame and the National Wrestling Hall of Fame. In 1996, he was listed as one of the top 100 U.S. Olympians of all time.

Now serving as the assistant to the athletic director at the University of Iowa, Gable continues to work with world-class wrestlers, overseeing their training in preparation for major national and international competitions. Gable keeps his home in Iowa City, and when not involved with Hawkeye athletics or national speaking engagements, he enjoys outdoor activities with his family, especially camping, boating, fishing, and wildlife sightseeing.

203